A KID'S GUIDE TO THE NAMES OF JESUS

TONY EVANS

HARVEST HOUSE PUBLISHERS
EUGENE, OREGON

Cover design by Left Coast Design

Cover illustration by Krieg Barrie

Interior design by Rockwell Davis

HARVEST KIDS is a trademark of The Hawkins Children's LLC. Harvest House Publishers, Inc., is the exclusive licensee of the trademark HARVEST KIDS.

A KID'S GUIDE TO THE NAMES OF JESUS

Copyright © 2021 by Tony Evans
Published by Harvest House Publishers
Eugene, Oregon 97408
www.harvesthousepublishers.com

ISBN 978-0-7369-7532-2 (pbk.)
ISBN 978-0-7369-7533-9 (eBook)

Printed in the United States of America

21 22 23 24 25 26 27 28 29 / BP-RD / 10 9 8 7 6 5 4 3 2 1

Contents

Introduction

The Fame of Jesus

What makes a person famous? Does being famous mean having a certain number of followers on social media? Do famous people need to star in blockbuster movies or release popular songs or appear on TV? And what about those who are super well known in their school or community—the people whose names *everyone* seems to know? Are they famous?

Everyone wants to be recognized. Everyone wants to be known by others. And some people do become famous—meaning that if someone says that person's name, others are going to instantly know who they are. In today's world of Instagram and YouTube and TikTok, average people who aren't athletes or musicians or actors can become famous if enough people start following them.

You might feel like you know your favorite celebrities—your favorite basketball player, your favorite musician, your favorite YouTuber—because you see their social media posts, talk about them with your friends, and feel like you know a lot about their lives. But while it *seems* like you know them, you actually only know *about* them—and only about what they choose to share with the public. You don't really know them, and they definitely don't know you!

Write down a list of your current favorite celebrities (authors, athletes, singers, actors, social media stars, and so on). Now, have a parent (or better yet, a grandparent!) make a list of their favorite all-time celebrities. (Important: Don't show each other your lists while you're writing them down!) After you make your lists, show them to each other. Do they know all your favorites? Do you know all of theirs? I'm guessing you might know some of each other's, but probably not all of them!

_____

_____

_____

_____

There are a lot of people in our world who we are very aware of because of their talents (like singing or acting), sports skills (like tennis or soccer), or social media presence (like fun YouTube videos). But did you know that in not very many years, no one will remember these people? New singers and actors will appear, athletes will get old and retire, and the fun YouTube videos will get boring. It might seem weird to imagine, but eventually nobody is going to know who these people were and what they did.

Even those who are famous for a longer time than normal will be remembered only when people read about them in history books or watch movies about them or learn about them in school. They won't be in the news or pop up on our screens every day.

Famous people may look impressive now. Their follower counts on social media may be massive. But in time, all of that will go away. For most celebrities, nobody will even remember their names.

There's one name, though, that people will never forget—and that's the name of Jesus.

Before we start learning about Jesus's names, can you think of any of those names on your own? Don't cheat and look ahead, but do try to think of Bible verses, songs you sing in church, and things you've learned about God at church camps or clubs. Write them down here.

_____

_____

_____

_____

Jesus never published a book, and yet there are more books written about Him (including this book!) than any other subject...*ever*. He never wrote a song, and yet more songs are written about Him than any about other person who lived. He never physically traveled more than 300 miles (which is shorter than the distance from Los Angeles to San Francisco) from the place where He was born, and yet there's no place on earth you can go where people don't know His name. And more and more people keep learning who Jesus is even though He's been physically gone from this earth for more than 2,000 years.

Jesus is a unique celebrity. Stores make a lot of money during the month of His birthday. (Christmas!) Family gatherings take place all around the world in celebration of His resurrection. (Easter!) All four books of the Bible known as the Gospels—Matthew, Mark, Luke, and John— tell the story of His birth. The Bible tells us why Jesus is the only person who ever lived on earth who should be known as a true celebrity: "Being in very nature God, [Jesus] did not consider equality with God something to be used to his own advantage; rather, he made himself nothing by taking the very nature of a servant, being made in human likeness" (Philippians 2:6-7).

Many celebrities travel with an entourage—a group of people who help them by doing everything from ordering food to protecting them from crazy fans. Most of the time, celebrities like to keep some distance from their fans. They need a little space from the people who are crowding in to get an autograph or take a picture with them. Attention can be fun, but too much attention can be overwhelming!

Jesus isn't like that. Even though He's the biggest celebrity of all time, we can get as close to Him as we want to. We can spend as much time as we like in His presence. He always makes time for us. And by knowing Him, we can receive some pretty good stuff—things that are way better than autographs or selfies.

As you get to know some of Jesus's names and titles, learn more about what it means to follow Him, and maybe even choose to become one of His followers, you will discover how amazing it is to know personally the most famous individual of all time—Jesus.

Write down the first ten words that come to mind when you think of Jesus.

1. _____   6. _____

2. _____   7. _____

3. _____   8. _____

4. _____   9. _____

5. _____   10. _____

Immanuel

When you say a person's name, you are referring to their *identity,* or who they are. If you were to walk up to a group of people you know and ask to speak to Amanda, Amanda would be the one who answered. It wouldn't be Jared. Or Karli. Or Devon. The reason why Amanda would answer is because that is her name. That is her *identity*. It is not Jared's or Karli's or Devon's or anyone else's identity.

Back in Bible times, names were given as early as possible— often before the baby was born—because parents wanted their child's name to reflect what they wanted their child to become. For example, the name Rebecca means "servant of God." And the name Noah means "peaceful" or "restful."

You probably have three names—a first name, a middle name, and a last name. Maybe you have another name, like a hyphenated last name or more than one middle name. But most people just go by one name (usually their first name). But God has a lot of names. Why is that?

God goes by a lot of different names because each name has its own important meaning. And He needs a lot of names to reflect His amazing characteristics. Each name tells us something new about God and helps us get to know Him better. Each name also helps us understand what He does, how He relates to us, and how He helps us. This might seem kind of complicated and overwhelming right now—after all, don't you have enough to memorize in school without worrying about memorizing even more? But learning the names of God is fun and totally worth it!

Look up the meaning of your own name and also the names of your best friends and family members. What does everyone's name mean? Do you think the meaning fits the person?

Name

Meaning

Not only does God the Father go by many meaningful names, but Jesus—God the Son—has a number of names Himself. (Deep breath here—you've got this!) Before we dive deeply into this whole name thing, though, let's set the stage and go back in time more than 2,000 years to the day Jesus was welcomed into this world. Yep, we're going back to Bethlehem and the very first Christmas Day.

The Best Birthday

Are you familiar with the British royal family? Whenever a new baby is about to be born into the royal family, it's a very big deal. Everybody talks about the coming arrival and guesses whether the new baby will be a boy or a girl and what his or her name will be.

Where were you born? Ask your family to tell you all about the day you were born. What happened? How did everyone feel? Who came to visit you after you were born? How does your own birth seem different from what you know about how and where Jesus was born?

_____

_____

_____

_____

_____

Even though Jesus came into this world as a King and could have been born in a castle like a royal baby, that's not what God chose to have happen. Not at all! Jesus wasn't born in a castle to parents whose names the whole world knew. Nope! Jesus was born in a barn to parents who were unknown and poor. Nobody sent Him flowers. No nurse helped change His diapers. The few gifts He would receive would come much later.

Write down what you think a miracle is. Can you think of any miracles from the Bible?

_____

_____

_____

_____

_____

But Jesus's birth was super important because He is the only One who ever lived who was both fully God and fully human. I know that seems incredibly hard to understand, but it's true. His birth was a miracle, and it only could have happened to the Son of God. During His time on earth, so many amazing things occurred that could have happened only to God's Son. Jesus felt hunger because He was fully human, yet He would later feed 5,000 because He was also fully God (Luke 9:10-17). He knew what it was like to be thirsty because He was fully human, yet He would one day walk on water because He was fully God (John 6:16-21). He learned things from His parents because He was fully human, but He also knew all about other people because He was fully God (Matthew 9:3-4).

Jesus's birth was like nobody else's birth because He was fully God and fully human. That had never happened before, and it will never happen again.

The Angel's Announcement

You might remember the story of what happened to Jesus's mother, Mary, before Jesus was born. She received a visit from the angel Gabriel, who told her she would have a son who would also be the Son of God. This must have seemed pretty crazy to Mary! She wasn't yet married to her future husband, Joseph, and she was young and poor and had no idea she would be chosen as the mother of God here on earth. But because Mary trusted in God and chose to obey Him, she accepted her role as the mother of Jesus. It probably helped a lot when Gabriel explained why she didn't have to be afraid: "The Lord is with you...You have found favor with God" (see Luke 1:28-30).

The angel also told Mary about the special role Jesus would play in history—and for all eternity. "He will be great and will be called the Son of the Most High. The Lord God will give him the throne of his father David, and he will reign over Jacob's descendants forever; his kingdom will never end" (verses 32-33).

Jesus was born in a barn to poor parents, but He came to reign in power and glory as King. It makes no sense at all, but it's true!

Mary didn't doubt the angel's announcement, but she did ask one important question: "How?" (see Luke 1:34). She didn't question God's power or ability, but she *was* confused about how this was all going to work. We all would be!

The angel Gabriel responded, "The Holy Spirit will come on you, and the power of the Most High will overshadow you" (verse 35). Basically, the angel told Mary, "God's gonna do a miracle—you just need to say yes!" And Mary did.

"For to us a child is born, to us a son is given" (Isaiah 9:6). Let's talk about that word "given." The Son was given by God. As the Son of God, Jesus already existed, but He came to earth in human form as a baby. A lot of people like to limit the Christmas story to baby Jesus in the manger because it's crazy to think of a baby being the Son of God and a King—but that's the most important part of the whole story. And even though Jesus was just a baby at His birth, He was already God. That's why the Son had to be "given" to us.

Jesus Gets Us

Jesus came to earth as the Son of God so that we could know God and understand that He walked around in our world. He got to know what it was like to be us—to deal with hunger and thirst and happiness and sadness and joy and pain.

Jesus could have been born in a castle with special messengers announcing that He was a King and that everyone had to follow Him. But here's the problem with that: Most of us can't identify with kings and queens and princes and princesses. Or anyone else who is super famous. Or super rich. Or super popular. That's why God decided Jesus would be born in a barn in a small town to unknown parents. And the world He was born into had a lot of problems and didn't always seem safe. Those are things that normal, everyday people (like you and me) can relate to. We can feel like Jesus was one of us—because He was.

Look around you. Write down everything you see in nature—trees, clouds, birds, flowers...even your dog! All of these things were created by God, and all of these things help reveal God's amazing power.

_____

_____

_____

_____

_____

God gave us a Savior we could understand. In understanding Him and getting to know His names, we get to know and understand God more too. John 1:18 says, "No one has ever seen God, but the one and only Son, who is himself God and is in closest relationship with the Father, has made him known."

If anybody ever walks up to you and says, "Hey, I have seen God with my own eyes!" that person is just making up a story or might be extremely confused. The Bible tells us very clearly that no one has ever seen God. Our flimsy human bodies weren't made to stand in the presence of God's glory. It's like staring straight into the sun. It can't and shouldn't be done. There's too much power there for a direct stare. We'll go completely blind if we try it.

So how could God show us Himself without vaporizing us? Answer: He shows Himself in Jesus. To see Jesus is to see God.

Have you ever wanted something out of a high cupboard or off of a tall shelf but couldn't reach it on your own? Either you had to stand on a chair to reach it or you needed someone taller to get it for you. That's how it worked with Jesus coming to earth. Jesus took everything there was to know about God and put it on a lower shelf—one we could reach.

Did you know that God and Jesus are completely connected? You can't have one without the other. You can't skip Jesus and have God. You can't say that you don't believe in Jesus but you do believe in God. It just doesn't work that way. Jesus is *God with us*. In fact, that's what the name Immanuel means—"God with us."

God with Us

Do you know what a master key is? It's a key that's made to unlock more than one door. Maybe you have one key for the front door of your house and another key for the back door. A master key would unlock both the front and back doors.

You can think of Jesus as your master key to God Himself. Jesus unlocks the heart and mind and nature of God. And it is through Jesus that we get to know God, learn about His power, and understand how much He loves us. Without Jesus, we could never come to know God.

The best name for understanding how God feels about us is the first name we're learning about: Immanuel. We see this name in Matthew 1:22-23, and it sets the stage for all the names to follow:

> All this took place to fulfill what the Lord had said through the prophet: "The virgin will conceive and

give birth to a son, and they will call him Immanuel" (which means "God with us").

Those two Bible verses tell us the meaning of Immanuel: "God with us." The importance of this name can be traced back to the Old Testament, when God's people—the nation of Israel—were being attacked by a huge enemy army. The King of Israel couldn't see any way his people were going to win, and all the Israelites were full of fear, anxiety, and dread. That's when God showed up and told the king that victory was coming. Immanuel, or "God with us," was on the way.

Never Alone

When we think of Christmas, we think of the baby Jesus and hot chocolate with peppermint sticks, Christmas carols, and brightly wrapped presents under the tree. Christmas feels cozy and warm and happy. And it is. But the baby Jesus—Immanuel—is also a source of comfort during the really hard and scary times.

Here's one thing I want you to always remember: No matter how scared or anxious or sad you are, Jesus is always with you. No matter how much you're struggling in school or how alone you feel or how frustrated you get with your life, God is with you. No matter how many problems your family is having or how frightened you are about what you hear on the news, God is with you.

No matter what you're going through, *you are never alone*. When your schoolwork is hard, you are not alone. When kids bully you, you are not alone. When your family is fighting, you are not alone. Jesus is *always* with you.

Think of a time when you had to do something really hard or when something made you super sad or upset. What happened? Who helped you? You can always count on God to help you in any situation!

_____

_____

_____

_____

_____

When we talk about Jesus—Immanuel—we are talking about someone who was fully God *and* fully human when He walked on this earth. That's what "God with us" means. And Jesus is God with us in every way. He has come as Immanuel—"God with us"—to show us more about God than we could have known any other way. If you're ever confused about who God is and what He is like, all you have to do is remember Immanuel.

You might wonder why God sent Immanuel to us instead of just showing us Himself as He is. This is a pretty hard thing to understand, but let's give it a go. God is *transcendent*—which basically means He's too big for our physical world to contain. It's like He lives in a different dimension than we do, another zone that we can't see. And yet God is also *immanent*—He is right here with us, and He wants us to know that. And that's why He sent Jesus. When Immanuel was born, God stepped into our zone so we could see Him and know Him in a new way.

Because Jesus is both the Son of God and the Son of Man, we can't separate Jesus from God. From the beginning of the world to its end, there is no place you can look and not see God revealed through Jesus. He is everywhere! Colossians 1:17 says, "He is before all things, and in him all things hold together."

Choosing the Son

There was once a rich man who had lost his beloved son, and then later the rich man also died. The rich man had collected many expensive and valuable possessions that were to be sold in an auction following his death. A lot of people wanted to buy what he had owned, so hundreds of people showed up for this auction.

The first item the auctioneer presented for sale was a cheaply framed picture that nobody seemed to want. The auctioneer said, "The first piece we're selling today is this portrait of the rich man's son." He held up the picture for everyone to see and then asked, "Do I have a bid?"

The room fell silent. The auctioneer could tell that nobody was interested in the picture, but he asked once more, "Do I have a bid? Does anyone want this portrait of the man's son?"

From the back of the room, an elderly man stepped forward and said, "Sir, I worked for the man who died. If nobody wants to buy the picture of his son, I want to know if I can have it."

The auctioneer said, "One more time...Does anyone want

to bid on the picture of the son?" When nobody did, he said to the employee, "Yes, sir, the picture is yours."

The servant walked to the front of the room to take the portrait, and when the auctioneer handed it to him, something shocking happened. The auctioneer picked up his gavel, banged it down, and said to everyone in the room, "Thank you very much for coming. The auction is now over."

The people were stunned. What about all the costly items that were to be sold?

But the auctioneer had something more to say: "The man's will stated that the first item to be auctioned was the picture of his son and that whoever took the picture would get everything else. His son was so important to him that he wanted to reward anyone else who honored him."

The rich man in this story is like God, and the son is like Jesus. And we're like the people at the auction. If we want the picture of the Son, we get everything. But if we don't want the Son, we get nothing.

A lot of people are like the buyers at the auction. They're looking for things they think are expensive and valuable, like brand-name clothes and the latest technology. But God wants to give us something even better. He tells us, "I have come to give you life—a good life. But that good life can be found only in connection with My Son. If you have My Son, you have eternal life and all that goes with it." The Bible clearly states this: "He who did not spare his own Son, but gave him up for us all—how will he not also along with him graciously give us all things?" (Romans 8:32).

When you accept Jesus, you also accept the good life that God the Father has for you. And knowing and understanding the names of Jesus shows you more and more how to receive that good life. So let's get to know Jesus—Immanuel—and discover the good life God wants to give us (John 10:10).

The name Immanuel means "God with us." Write down the name and definition here so you can come back to it and remember it later. You can write it fancy or draw some pictures to help you remember it even better.

_____

_____

_____

_____

_____

_____

2

Alpha and Omega

When you're reading a book, where do you start? At the beginning, of course! It would make no sense to start halfway through or even ten or twenty pages in. If you did that, you would miss something. And the entire book probably wouldn't make as much sense.

Let's continue to look at the names of Jesus by starting at the beginning. Alpha is the first letter in the Greek alphabet. That's pretty easy to remember because *A* is the first letter in the English alphabet. Alpha is also one of Jesus's names. But before we get into that, let's take a quick look at the English alphabet.

The alphabet was one of the first things you were taught when you started school or when you were getting ready for school. When I was growing up, we sang songs that helped us memorize the alphabet. Today, there are lots of games, toys, and videos that help young kids learn the letters and their sounds.

Children need to learn the alphabet because knowing the letters from *A* to *Z* is the first step in learning how to read and write. Words depend on letters. Letters make up words. Our thoughts become words, and that's how we communicate with other people. It would be really hard to talk to another person without words, wouldn't it?

Imagine what your life would be like if you didn't know the alphabet. You wouldn't be able to read. You wouldn't be able to talk to your friends or text them. You wouldn't be able to tell jokes or play games with your family. It would be really hard!

The alphabet is important because letters matter. Words matter. Thoughts matter. And knowledge matters.

What are some ways you first learned the alphabet? If you can't remember, ask a parent or grandparent. They probably helped teach you!

_____

_____

_____

_____

_____

Now, what "*A* to *Z*" is in the English language, "alpha and omega" is in Greek. Alpha is the first letter of the Greek alphabet, and omega is the last. When Jesus lived on earth, He lived in a Greek-speaking world. He knew the letters alpha and omega and understood why they were important. So when Jesus calls Himself the Alpha and the Omega, He declares that He is everything from *A* to *Z*. He's the beginning and the end—and everything in between.

Jesus added that He is "the First and the Last" (Revelation 22:13). No letter comes before Him, and no letter comes after Him. He is the first, the last, and everything in between. By saying this, He's declaring that He is the living God. We know this because God referred to Himself in the same way in the Old Testament.

How does knowing the letters of the alphabet help you in life? What are some things you couldn't do if you didn't know the alphabet?

In Isaiah 44:6 we read, "This is what the LORD says—Israel's King and Redeemer, the LORD Almighty: I am the first and I am the last; apart from me there is no God." And Isaiah 48:12 says, "Listen to me, Jacob, Israel, whom I have called: I am he; I am the first and I am the last."

When Jesus declared He is the Alpha and the Omega, the first and the last, He affirmed that He is the God of the Old

Testament. Here's a question for you: How many firsts and lasts can there be? Just one first and just one last, right? So if the God of the Old Testament introduced Himself as the first and the last, then when Jesus describes Himself the same way, we know He is the same as God.

Jesus Is the Final Word

The only right way to create a word in the English language is to use letters in the English alphabet. Other letters can be used to create other words in other languages, but in order for the word to be an English word, you need to use the English alphabet. If someone creates a word not using the letters of the English alphabet, then that word will not be an English word. Similarly, Jesus has made it clear that He is the *totality*—or the whole amount—of all the letters from alpha to omega. Nothing can be created without Jesus. Anything created without Him simply won't be true.

Jesus isn't the *A* to *G* in our lives. We aren't supposed to think of Him only *some* of the time—like on Sunday morning or at Christmas and Easter. He is part of our lives and part of our world *all* the time. He is the ultimate Alpha and Omega, the beginning and the end, and everything in between. In the book of Colossians, the apostle Paul shows us that everything comes from Jesus:

- "The Son is the image of the invisible God, the firstborn over all creation" (1:15).

- "He is before all things, and in him all things hold together" (1:17).

- "For God was pleased to have all his fullness dwell in him" (1:19).

- "...in whom are hidden all the treasures of wisdom and knowledge" (2:3).
- "Christ is all, and is in all" (3:11).

Write down everything you do in a day. After you have written it down, go back and highlight or put a star by everything that Jesus should be involved in. How can you bring Jesus into more of your life?

_____

_____

_____

_____

Did you notice a word that was repeated in those verses? The word is "all." Jesus knows all. Jesus understands all. Jesus rules over all. Jesus is all. If something we think or say doesn't agree with what Jesus teaches, it's not true. No matter what you hear in books or online or in songs or in TV shows or movies or even from your best friend, if what you hear is different from what Jesus says, then what you're hearing is wrong.

There are two answers to every question: God's answer and everybody else's. And when everybody else disagrees with God, everybody else is wrong.

Hebrews 12:25 tells us, "See to it that you do not refuse him who speaks." We are not to ignore or refuse to hear what Jesus says. And we need to take the time to find out what Jesus is telling us.

Besides *knowing* what Jesus says, we also need to *obey* what He says. In fact, God tells us that when we don't listen to Jesus and follow His commands, He will shake up our lives in order to get our attention (see Hebrews 12:10-11). And in Hebrews 1:2, we read, "In these last days [God] has spoken to us by his Son, whom he appointed heir of all things, and through whom also he made the universe." This means that Jesus isn't just the final word on church things; He is the final word on *all* things—friendships, school, entertainment, ideas, activities...everything!

A great Christian writer named C.S. Lewis (he wrote The Chronicles of Narnia and other amazing books) said that you can believe in the sun not just because you see it but also because you see everything else because of it. Similarly, we are not only to believe in Jesus but also to view everything in life through His eyes. Jesus is our sun, and it's because of Him that we see everything. To make it really simple, whatever Jesus says, goes.

Have you ever been complaining or arguing and your mom or dad says, "Didn't you hear what I just said?" The bottom line is that your mom or dad has said the final word, and complaining or arguing won't change anything. The topic is no longer up for discussion.

The same goes for anything that Jesus says. Jesus is the final word. Period.

A Strong Finish

You can accomplish so many amazing things if you decide to live by Jesus's truth! You can finish the race and fulfill the purpose God has created you to live out. Hebrews 12:1-3 explains this:

Since we are surrounded by such a great cloud of witnesses, let us throw off everything that hinders and the sin that so easily entangles. And let us run with perseverance the race marked out for us, fixing our eyes on Jesus, the pioneer and perfecter of faith. For the joy set before him he endured the cross, scorning its shame, and sat down at the right hand of the throne of God. Consider him who endured such opposition from sinners, so that you will not grow weary and lose heart.

What are your favorite sports to watch in the Olympics?

_____

_____

_____

_____

Have you ever been running and felt like you just wanted to stop? This could happen when you're actually running, or it could happen when you're "running" in another way. You might be tired of school. Maybe this year you don't have good friends in your classes, or you just don't connect with your teacher. You might be tired of how things are going at home. Maybe you argue a lot with your siblings, or your mom or dad just lost their job and things aren't as happy as they used to be. Maybe you're feeling a lot of anxiety about your friendships or the future or just life in general. But even though things might be rough right now, don't quit. Jesus is with you, and He promises to help you cross the finish line.

You have a race to finish—a race of living your life for the glory of God and the good of yourself and others. And even though sometimes you might want to drop out of the race, Jesus will come alongside you and help you finish strong.

Even if a gymnast falls off the balance beam or a runner trips and falls, they can still get up and finish the competition—and maybe even win! For an inspiring example, go online with your parents and search "Heather Dorniden" on YouTube.

_____

_____

_____

_____

You have the power to keep going because Jesus has the power to both start and finish whatever it is you might face. And the way to keep going is to focus your attention on Jesus.

When you focus on something, you naturally stop focusing on anything else. It's not possible to focus on many things at the same time. To focus on Jesus is to zero in on Him. You stop paying so much attention to your friends' opinions or what the world says. You look at Jesus and Him alone.

Where you look determines where you will go. Ballet dancers do this when they turn. It's called "spotting." By focusing on one spot, they can turn without getting dizzy. Basketball players do this when they shoot with good follow-through and their hand points down toward the basket. If you look in the right direction, you will go in the right direction.

You can see a great example of this in the Bible in Matthew 14:22-31. In this passage, we read about the time when a great storm hit the sea, and Jesus walked to His disciples on the rough water. Jesus had sent them out into the bad weather. The problem was the storm. But when Jesus came to the disciples, He walked on top of the very problem itself. He didn't get rid of the storm; He overcame it. He overpowered it.

One of the disciples, Peter, asked if he could join Jesus out on the water. As long as Peter looked at Jesus, he was fine. But when he took his eyes off Jesus and instead focused on the storm, Peter began to sink.

If we choose to focus on Jesus as Peter did, we will have the power to overcome any storm.

The apostle Paul told some of his friends, "I thank my God every time I remember you...being confident of this, that he who began a good work in you will carry it on to completion until the day of Christ Jesus" (Philippians 1:3,6). That is such great news! If you focus on Him, He can take you to the finish line.

In the sport of rowing, one member of the team is called the "coxswain." This is the person who sits in the stern of the boat. The people who do the rowing face toward the back. They can't see where they're going. All they can see is the coxswain. This person tells the rowers what to do—how fast to row and when to pull harder on the oars. If the rowers were to turn around and take their attention off the coxswain, they would lose time—and in a race, every second counts. Only when the rowers focus their attention on the one giving instructions do they have a chance of winning.

Life isn't always perfect. We don't always get straight As or have perfect friendships or win things. Yet when we choose to focus on Jesus and live our lives by His words and His truth, He will help us. He is the Alpha and the Omega. He is the beginning and the end. He is the first and the last. Jesus promises to get you across that finish line. You'll always finish the race—and win—with Jesus.

The name "Alpha and Omega" means "the beginning and the end—and everything in between." Write down the name and definition here so you can come back to it and remember it later. You can write it fancy or draw some pictures to help you remember it even better.

_____

_____

_____

3

King

f someone came over to my house and started using bad words or acting like a bully or fighting and arguing, I would not allow that person to continue doing those things. That's because in my house, everyone must follow certain rules.

You've probably experienced the same thing. Your parents have set rules that everyone who lives in your home or comes to visit must follow. Your teacher has certain rules for your classroom. Your coach has certain rules for your team. They're in charge, and their rules are the ones everyone has to follow.

My daughter Chrystal has a very strong heart and mind. She knows what she wants to do, and that strength has given her the ability to go far in life. But when she was younger and still living at home, that strength sometimes collided with my own. One day Chrystal came to me arguing about something, and the argument went on for some time. When Chrystal saw that I wasn't going to give in, she started to walk away while I was still talking to her. I quickly asked, "Where do you think you are going?"

She replied, "I'm going to my room!"

To which I said, "You are not going to your room, because that is not your room. That is my room, and I let you sleep in it. And right now, you cannot go there."

What are some rules that everyone who lives in or visits your home has to follow? What about rules in your classroom? Or rules at your favorite activity (the gym where you play basketball, the dance studio, or the building where your choir practices)? What happens when someone breaks those rules?

_____

_____

_____

_____

_____

Chrystal had a wrong view of the room she used in my house. She didn't own it; I allowed her to use it. As the parent, I paid the bills and provided what she needed. And yet Chrystal wanted to argue about my rules. She wanted me to adjust my rules, but it was my house. And as a responsible parent, I couldn't give in. I had established loving guidelines and boundaries for everyone who lived in my house, and those boundaries helped my children to learn respect, self-control, and obedience.

God's House

God also has a house—His kingdom. Psalm 24:1 tells us, "The earth is the LORD's, and everything in it, the world, and all who live in it."

God created His world, so He gets to run it the way He wants to. He makes the rules. If you want to make your own rules, go make your own world. In this one, God rules. I call God's rule the "kingdom agenda." In the kingdom agenda, God is in control, and we need to follow His lead. The Bible shows us how this works:

- "In the beginning God created the heavens and the earth" (Genesis 1:1).

- "Then the LORD God formed a man from the dust of the ground and breathed into his nostrils the breath of life, and man became a living being" (Genesis 2:7).

- "The LORD God took the man and put him in the Garden of Eden to work it and take care of it" (Genesis 2:15).

- "What is mankind that you are mindful of them, human beings that you care for them? You have made them a little lower than the angels and crowned them with glory and honor. You made them rulers over the works of your hands; you put everything under their feet" (Psalm 8:4-6).

- "The highest heavens belong to the LORD, but the earth he has given to mankind" (Psalm 115:16).

God created people to run His house His way. Yet Adam and Eve made some bad choices and weren't able to do the job—and no other human after them could do the job either. So God had to provide someone else, and that someone else was Jesus Christ.

The Old Testament part of the Bible includes a lot of verses that tell of the coming of Jesus, like this one:

> Rejoice greatly, Daughter Zion! Shout, Daughter Jerusalem! See, your king comes to you, righteous and victorious, lowly and riding on a donkey, on a colt, the foal of a donkey (Zechariah 9:9).

The Christmas story is the fulfillment of Old Testament prophecy and the coming of the King—Jesus. Write down the Christmas story in your own words or draw a picture of it.

_____

_____

_____

We shouldn't be surprised that when Jesus was ready to show the world He was King, He told His disciples to get a donkey, since that was what the Old Testament said he would ride into Jerusalem. You know how there's a lot of excitement about the release of a new Disney movie or the next book in a popular series? That's what was happening here. People had been looking forward to the King's coming for a long time!

The King's Rules

When we speak of Jesus, one of the names we aren't so quick to call Him by is King. We think of Jesus as our Savior and friend and helper—and He *is* all of those things! But sometimes we forget that Jesus is King, and if we forget that, we miss out on His power. This power shows up in names like King, Lord, and Great High Priest.

When we recognize Jesus as King, we also have to act like He is our King. And that means we need to obey Him, depend on Him, honor Him, and respect Him. You probably aren't used to living life under a king, and it might seem a little weird, but living life under a *good* king is a good thing— and living life under the *best* King is the best thing!

A lot of the problems in our world—and in our own lives— come from not living according to the King's laws. If we decide to make our own rules and do our own thing, it's not going to work out very well. There will be consequences for our actions.

You know that there are consequences when you break the rules at home or at school, right? If you fight with your brother, you might get assigned extra chores. If you don't hand in your homework, your grade will go down. If Jesus gave us an extra chore or a bad grade every time we disobeyed one of His commands, we might learn a little faster how to obey. But He is patient with us and allows us to make mistakes. And He helps us learn to obey when we ask Him for help.

Have your parents ever told you what to do and you decided to argue about it? They tell you what they want— for you to do the dishes, for example—and then you give them your opinion. Maybe you have homework to do, or you think it's your sister's turn to do the dishes. It would probably take less effort just to go ahead and do the dishes, but you don't want to, so you argue about it.

We do the same thing with God, probably more than we realize. We say that Jesus is King and that we're part of His kingdom, yet we argue His truth and disobey His commands. But as King, Jesus has the final say-so on every single subject. And as His disciples, we are not only to spread the gospel of His kingdom (Matthew 24:14) but also to live it out in our own lives.

Who are some people who have power in your life (parents, teachers, other leaders, and so on)? Who has power over all of these people? (Hint: He's a King!) What can you do to obey them and also obey the King?

_____

_____

_____

_____

Putting the King First

Our role as Jesus's disciples involves more than sharing with others how He can save them and they can go to heaven. We also need to be examples of how to live for Jesus here on earth. When someone trusts Jesus as their personal Savior, that gets them into heaven. And when they start living their lives under His kingdom rule, they have access to His amazing power!

You probably don't mind following rules when you agree with them. But if a rule seems unfair or silly, you probably *do* mind following it. Many of us don't mind following Jesus's rules when we agree with Him, but we don't want to when we disagree.

For example, Jesus has told us to love our neighbor. (Our neighbor can be anyone we meet in life.) It's easy to love someone who is nice, but it's hard to love someone who is mean. Yet we need to follow Jesus's rules *no matter what*—and so we need to love both the nice person and the mean person.

When I was a kid and argued with my dad, he liked to say, "Son, you haven't lived here long enough to know how to call the shots." When it comes to Jesus our King, He calls the shots.

When you accept Jesus Christ as your Savior, you also accept Him as King in your life. You are to follow what He says, not what the crowd says. It doesn't matter how many people like or dislike your decisions or how many people argue with you or put you down—none of that matters. The only question that matters is, "What does the King say?" Because He rules.

Matthew 6:33 tells us to seek first God's kingdom and His righteousness, and everything else will fall into place. Luke 12:31-32 says, "Seek his kingdom, and these things will be given to you as well. Do not be afraid, little flock, for your Father has been pleased to give you the kingdom." This means that God is thrilled to give you the kingdom when you put Him first.

Many people assume that if they just get closer to Jesus, they will always automatically do the right thing. And while getting closer to Jesus is super important, it doesn't mean you will become perfect just like that. You need to spend time learning about His rules. Yes, Jesus loves you. Yes, Jesus comforts you. Yes, Jesus provides for you. But Jesus also rules over you.

Heavenly Passport

Lots of people want a Savior, but they don't want a King. They don't want Jesus Christ calling the shots or having the final say. But unless we let Him call the shots and have the final say, our lives are going to be a hot mess. The Bible says, "Our citizenship is in heaven. And we eagerly await a Savior from there, the Lord Jesus Christ" (Philippians 3:20). This means that if you have accepted Jesus as your Savior, you are first and foremost a citizen of heaven.

Make yourself a passport, even if you haven't yet been out of your country (or even your state). Write down "heaven" as your place of citizenship, and then make a list of all the countries, states, or cities you've visited (or you'd like to visit!).

PASSPORT

Photograph

Name

Signature

Passport Number:

Description:

Gender:

Age:

Country:

If you travel to another country, you need to carry a passport. That passport allows you to leave your own country—the place where you are a citizen—and enter another country. A passport lets you visit other countries or kingdoms. The passport confirms who you are and where you live—where you are a citizen—so that many of the rules of your own country will apply to you no matter what country you are visiting.

If you are a citizen of heaven—as everyone who believes in Jesus is—Jesus does not expect you to leave your heavenly passport at home. When you go to school, hang out with friends, or do stuff online, Jesus does not want you to pretend to be someone else. You are part of the kingdom of heaven, and you need to follow the rules of that kingdom.

What is your role in Jesus's kingdom? What are some things you can do to show that you are one of His subjects and that you want to live your life for Him?

_____

_____

_____

_____

Jesus is King. He is our ruler. He is the final authority, and He calls the shots. Matthew 28:18 says, "Jesus came to them and said, 'All authority in heaven and on earth has been given to me.'" Not some. Not part. Not a little bit, but *all*.

Since all authority belongs to Jesus, don't you think it would be wise to obey Him? He's in charge—of everything. Even the things you struggle with. Even the people who don't like you. Even the things that don't seem fair.

Jesus is King over *all*. That's why you don't have to be afraid of anything. It doesn't matter if someone has better grades, more popularity, a better singing voice, or more athletic ability than you have. Everyone is all together under Jesus. He is the King, and nobody is more important than Him.

No human being has the last word over you, because no human being is the King of kings. They may be *a* king, but they are not *the* King. They may be *a* leader, but they are not *the* leader. They may be *a* coach, but they are not *the* coach. Jesus is powerful and mighty, and He is always on your side. He's your general, chief, warrior, leader, and most importantly, your King.

"King" is yet another name or title for Jesus. Write down the name here so you can come back to it and remember it later. You can write it fancy or draw some pictures to help you remember it even better.

_____

_____

4

Lamb of God

It doesn't make sense for a king to also be a lamb, does it? Isn't a lamb meek and mild? We think of lambs as mini-sheep—cute but helpless animals that aren't very smart and just follow the big sheep around. Yet one of the names of Jesus is the Lamb of God. This might seem crazy, but the Lamb of God is actually a fierce and mighty King. In fact, this is the name you should call on when you're going through your toughest times.

Do you remember way back at the beginning of the Bible when Adam and Eve sinned in the Garden of Eden? And do you remember what they did right after they sinned? They didn't say, "Hey, God, we messed up! Come help us out!" No, they tried to fix the problem themselves. They even sewed some fig leaves together and tied those around their bodies to try to cover their shame. But that didn't work. They couldn't just hide from God and pretend that nothing had happened.

When you think of a lamb, what do you think of? Write down every word you can think of to describe a lamb.

_____

_____

_____

_____

What happened next is a little hard to understand, especially if you're an animal lover. But it's the way things worked back in the Old Testament. To cover Adam and Eve's sin, God had to sacrifice an animal (see Genesis 3:7,21). This act led to an entire system of sacrifices that took place throughout the whole Old Testament. Maybe you've read some of the stories where people had to bring an animal sacrifice to God.

The main part of the sacrificial system was an event called the Passover, which you can read about in Exodus 12. When the people of Israel were planning to leave Egypt, God told them to take the blood of a lamb and paint it on the doorposts of their home. This was to save the lives of the firstborn children of the Israelites. When the Lord came by each Israelite home, He would recognize the sacrifice and pass over that home, sparing everyone inside.

Taking Care of Sin

Because God is holy and fair and just, He doesn't just lose it and get mad when we sin. And while He doesn't prefer anger (or wrath, as the Bible often says), He can't skip justice.

He has to do *something*. He can't just let things go. But God also is filled with mercy and grace, so He came up with a plan.

The plan in the Old Testament—which was never intended to last forever because God had a bigger and better plan coming—involved sacrificing a lamb as well as other approved sacrifices. Every sacrifice needed to be spotless and sinless. It had to be perfect, without disease. It couldn't have anything wrong with it. And in a way, the sacrifice would be sinless—as an animal, it wouldn't have willfully participated in mankind's rebellion against God.

Now, this is a lot to understand, but here's the most important part to remember: God must judge sin. And we are sinful. Therefore, we're all under judgment. Nobody is going to get away with anything. And it doesn't matter whether you are a big sinner, a medium sinner, or a tiny sinner. No sin is okay, and every sin needs to be judged—or forgiven.

Some people think that because they obey most of the Ten Commandments, they should be okay. But imagine you were hanging by a chain over the side of a cliff, and the chain had ten links. If only one link breaks, what happens to you? You fall off the cliff! This is similar to what happens if you break only one of the Ten Commandments. You're no longer perfect. And God's standard is perfection, not just "okay."

First Corinthians 5:7 calls Jesus "our Passover lamb." John 1:29 tells us, "The next day John saw Jesus coming toward him and said, 'Look, the Lamb of God, who takes away the sin of the world!'" Jesus came as the Lamb of God, so His death on the cross covered the sin of every person who ever lived—and who will ever live.

Even though everyone's sins have been paid for through

Jesus's death on the cross, not everyone chooses to follow Jesus and receive eternal life. John 3:16 tells us, "For God so loved the world that he gave his one and only Son, that whoever believes in him shall not perish but have eternal life." If someone chooses not to accept Jesus as their personal Savior, they choose not to accept the life He offers them.

Can you remember the Ten Commandments? Write down the ones you remember, then look up any you can't remember. Have you ever broken any of them? (It's impossible not to!)

_____

_____

_____

_____

_____

_____

_____

_____

_____

Have you ever been given a birthday gift and then tried to pay the person who gave the gift to you? Or has anyone ever done that to you? I doubt it! Why? Because a gift is just that—a *gift*. It's the same with the gift of eternal life Jesus gives us. It's not something we can pay back. But we do need to accept the gift by placing our faith in Jesus and believing in Him.

If you accept Jesus's gift of eternal life, you will go to heaven. If you don't, you won't. God makes this very clear (see Revelation 20:11-15). The gospel is the "good news." You don't have to pay for any of it! The Bible says, "God made him who had no sin to be sin for us, so that in him we might become the righteousness of God" (2 Corinthians 5:21). That is such great news!

What good news have you received recently? Maybe you did really well on a school assignment or went on a fun trip or starred in a play. Always look for the good news in life! And always remember the *great* news—Jesus gives you eternal life!

_____

_____

_____

_____

Believing in Jesus

If you already believe in Jesus, you might be tempted to skip over this section. But I want you to read it even if you are already a Christian. If you aren't sure if you are a Christian or want to know more about what it means to follow Jesus, you should definitely read it. And if you are already a Christian, you should also definitely read it because it will help you learn how to share your faith with others.

The Problem

"All have sinned and fall short of the glory of God" (Romans 3:23).

Salvation is good news, but the bad news is that we're all sinners. Nobody is perfect. Everyone has sinned at least once.

It doesn't matter if you've sinned one time or a million times. Anytime you do something that goes against what God has told you to do, you've sinned. You're not perfect. And you fall short of the glory of God.

> Write down some of the ways you have sinned in the past day or week. Now pray and ask God to forgive those sins. Finally, erase them or cross them out because God has forgiven you!
>
> _____
>
> _____
>
> _____

There's a story about two men who were exploring an island when a volcano suddenly erupted. In moments, the two found themselves surrounded by molten lava. Several feet away was a clearing—a path to safety. To get there, however, they would have to jump across the river of melted rock. The first man was very old and couldn't move quickly. He ran as fast as he could and jumped as far as he could, but he didn't make it and fell into the superheated lava.

The second man was younger and in much better shape. In fact, he was a college record-holder in the long jump. He put all his energy into his run, jumped with flawless form, and shattered his own college record. Unfortunately, he, too, landed far short of the clearing and fell into the hot lava.

It didn't matter that one man jumped farther than the other—neither one could jump far enough.

Like the two explorers, nobody is good enough to "outjump" the glory of God. We've all sinned, and we all fall short of His standard of perfection.

The Penalty

"Sin entered the world through one man, and death through sin, and in this way death came to all people, because all sinned" (Romans 5:12).

After reading this verse, you may be thinking, *It's not fair for the rest of us to suffer the consequences of Adam's sin!* But we suffer those consequences not only because Adam sinned but also because we sinned too.

Have you ever noticed that kids don't need to be taught how to sin? Maybe you have watched a younger sibling or even done some babysitting. Imagine sitting down with a little kid and saying, "Here's how to lie," or "Let me show you how to be selfish." That would be ridiculous—those things just come naturally!

Basically, sin is inside each of us at birth. It might take some time for that sin to be seen, but it's there and eventually makes its presence known. And sin demands a penalty, or punishment. That penalty, according to the Bible, is death (see Romans 6:23). Don't worry though—good news is on the way!

The Provision

"God demonstrates his own love for us in this: While we were still sinners, Christ died for us" (Romans 5:8).

This is the good news! God is more powerful than any sin, and He can make any situation right.

Even while we were still sinners, God proved His love for us by sending Jesus Christ, His righteous Lamb, to die in our place. How amazing that God would love us so deeply!

It's important to understand that not just *anyone* could die for the penalty of sin. All of us have sinned, so whoever would save us would have to be perfectly sinless.

Let me tell you another story. Two brothers were playing in the woods one summer day when, almost without warning, a bee stung the older brother on the eyelid. He put his hands to his face and fell to the ground in pain.

As the younger brother looked on in horror, the bee began buzzing around his head. Terrified, he began screaming, "The bee's going to get me too!"

The older brother, who had calmed down by now, said, "What are you talking about? That bee can't hurt you. He's already stung me."

Basically, this is what happened when Jesus died on the cross. He loves you so much that He stepped out of heaven and took the "stinger of death" in your place. Because Jesus Christ is without sin, His death paid the penalty for all of us (2 Corinthians 5:21).

The Pardon

If doing good things—like being nice to people or doing your brother's chores—could save you, there would have been no point in Jesus's death. But Jesus knew that no matter how many good things we did, we couldn't pay sin's price. That's why His sacrifice as the Lamb of God needed to happen. And in order for Him to save us, we must trust in Him for our salvation.

There's a difference between believing *in* Jesus and believing *about* Jesus. You can know a lot *about* Jesus— facts about His life that you can read about in the Bible. But to believe *in* Jesus, you need to totally trust in Him.

Think about what happens every time you sit down in a chair. The moment you decide to sit down, you trust that the chair will hold you up. If the chair looks iffy, though, you might steady yourself by grabbing something or resting only part of your weight on the chair. That's what some people do with Jesus. They're pretty sure Jesus is who He says He is, but instead of putting all their trust in Him, they also put their trust in other things, like good behavior, going to church, or reading their Bibles. Now, don't get me wrong. Those are all really good things to do. But they aren't going to save you. Only putting 100 percent trust in Jesus will do that.

You don't need to depend on anything other than Jesus for your salvation because He is enough. In fact, He's *more* than enough! You can express your faith in Jesus in prayer.

Jesus—the Lamb of God—died not only so we would have eternal life in heaven but also so we would have a good life here on earth. A good life doesn't mean a perfect life, but a life lived for God. And that is the *best* kind of life!

"Lamb" is yet another name for Jesus. Write down the name here so you can come back to it and remember it later. You can write it fancy or draw some pictures to help you remember it even better.

_____

_____

_____

_____

_____

_____

_____

5

Great High Priest

We've learned some of Jesus's most important names: Immanuel. The Alpha and Omega. Our King. The mighty Lamb.

It's time for another name of Jesus: Great High Priest. You probably aren't super familiar with this name, and that makes sense. This name is found in one of the hardest-to-understand books of the Bible—Hebrews. Hebrews can be confusing because it was written to people who knew quite a bit about the Old Testament. But most of us don't know a ton about the Old Testament. Maybe we have memorized some verses, but we haven't spent a lot of time studying that part of the Bible, like we have the New Testament and the life of Jesus.

I believe the main message of Hebrews can be summarized in three words: *Never give up.*

Hebrews was written to believers who were seriously

considering giving up on following Jesus. They were tempted to walk away from their faith. Living as a Christian in their culture was super difficult because they faced persecution (like being bullied but way worse!), tons of pressure, and a lot of other challenges. Life was really hard for those Christians, and that's why the author of Hebrews encouraged them not to quit.

What do you think it means to never give up? Can you think of a time when you wanted to give up but didn't? What happened?

_____

_____

_____

Even though you might be a Christian and go to church every Sunday and say your prayers and try your best to follow Jesus, there are times when your life also gets really hard. You wish you could just sleep in on a Sunday, or you want to do what your friends are doing even though you know their actions don't honor Jesus. But then you go to church and have a great time or you meet a new friend who follows Jesus, and you're encouraged again. That's why it's so important to never give up!

So What's a Priest?

Great High Priest might seem like a weird name or title for Jesus. It might sound more like something out of a history book or an adventure movie. But let's dig in and figure out exactly what it meant to be a priest in the Bible. And let's also see why Jesus goes by this name.

The Bible says that a priest had to be chosen from a group of men, which means that a priest had to be like the people he was serving. The priest also had to be appointed—or given his position—by God. He couldn't just wake up one morning and think, *Hey, I think I'll be a priest!* Also, nobody could just decide that someone else would be a priest. They couldn't just write a name on a ballot. There had to be a call from God saying, "This person is supposed to be a priest."

A priest also had to have another qualification, which we can read about in Hebrews 5:2: "He is able to deal gently with those who are ignorant and are going astray, since he himself is subject to weakness." The priest had to understand what it means to struggle. He needed to know what it felt like to have problems and issues. He needed to go through things so he could have compassion for others.

Write down what you learn in this chapter about being a priest. How did Jesus check all the boxes of what it meant to be a priest?

_____

_____

_____

If someone has never felt pain or sadness, it's hard for them to help people who are sad or hurting. When you are having a problem, it helps a ton to talk to someone who has dealt with the same problem.

All of these things give us a better idea of what it means for Jesus to be our Great High Priest. And Jesus met all the qualifications. Chosen from a group of men? *Check.* Called by God? *Check.* Knows what it means to struggle? *Check.* Jesus checked all the boxes.

What are some things in your life that aren't going so great right now? Jesus promises to be your anchor in the storms of life. You can pray and ask Him to hold you steady!

_____

_____

_____

_____

Jesus, our Great High Priest, came to help us with the hard things, make us stronger, and comfort us during the challenging and hard times. Jesus also brings us calmness and a connection with God. We can read about this in the book of Hebrews:

> We have this hope as an anchor of the soul, firm and secure. It enters the inner sanctuary behind the curtain, where our forerunner, Jesus, has entered on our behalf. He has become a high priest forever (6:19-20).

Jesus is the anchor for the soul. What does an anchor do? It holds a boat steady. When a sailor drops anchor, the anchor keeps the boat in place regardless of how windy or stormy it might be. Even though the boat may be rocking, it never leaves its location because the anchor holds it in place.

If you don't drop the anchor, that anchor does you no good. If you don't allow Jesus, the Great High Priest, to be your anchor, then the storms of life will carry you away until you eventually crash. When you look to Jesus as the Great High Priest, letting Him steady you along the way because you are securely tied to Him, then when things aren't working out at school or with your friends or on the soccer field, you will have an anchor. Jesus will hold you steady. He will give you hope.

When we have hope, we look forward to something good. What good things are you looking forward to right now?

_____

_____

_____

_____

What exactly is hope? Hope is joyful expectation about the future—like looking forward to a birthday celebration or a dance performance or summer camp. Hope is not concerned with where you are right now. Hope looks to where things are going to wind up. It always involves expectation and looking forward to something good.

Jesus Gets It

No one has ever experienced a difficulty in life that Jesus has not also experienced. He knows what it's like to be lonely. He knows what it's like to be rejected and to not fit in. He knows what it's like to be abandoned, physically beat up, and hurt. He knows how it feels to cry because the pain is so deep. He knows what it's like to have His friends turn on Him. He knows what it's like to be homeless. He knows what it's like to be thirsty and hungry. He knows what it's like to be tempted to do something wrong. He knows what it's like to be looked down on and made fun of. He even knows what it's like to feel the weight of the whole world's sin and to die on a cross.

Jesus gets it. He understands. He feels what you feel. That's why He's able to have so much compassion. Jesus will always give us mercy and grace to help us when we need Him to. But we have to do our part by coming to Him. Jesus promises to help you in your life and with your problems, but first you need to have a relationship with Him, the Great High Priest, and stay in close contact with Him.

You should never walk away from God if you are hurting. Instead, you need to run toward Him. Jesus gives you the strength to keep going even when life gets hard. When you walk with Jesus and stay connected to Him, you won't be tempted to give up. That's because Jesus, the Great High Priest, walks with you, always giving you the help you need.

"Great High Priest" is yet another name for Jesus. Write down the name here so you can come back to it and remember it later. You can write it fancy or draw some pictures to help you remember it even better.

_____

_____

_____

_____

_____

_____

6

Sovereign

There's a story about a bad storm that tore through the Midwest. People started scrambling for shelter, and as everyone was running around, a man saw a boy carrying another boy on his back. The boy being carried looked to be almost the size of the boy carrying him, but he was obviously younger. The man shouted, "That boy looks heavy! Do you need help?"

The boy doing the carrying replied, "Oh, he's not heavy. He's my brother!"

The boy was willing to go that extra mile—or two, or ten—out of love for his brother.

That same love is found in Jesus. But Jesus doesn't carry only one of us on His back. He carries *all* of us.

We all need Jesus to carry us through the storms life blows our way. Which is why the name we are going to look at in this chapter is so important. Immanuel, the name we learned at the start of this book, reminds us that God is with us. And the names King, Lamb, and Great High Priest reveal how God relates to us. But the next name shows us just how much God is for us—*for you*. He is on your side. He carries you. This name is Sovereign, which means He is ruler over all.

Write down all the names of Jesus you have learned so far. (Hint: Read the first sentence of this chapter!)

_____

_____

_____

_____

We can find this name—Sovereign—hinted at in Isaiah 9:6:

> For to us a child is born, to us a son is given, and the government will be on his shoulders. And he will be called Wonderful Counselor, Mighty God, Everlasting Father, Prince of Peace.

The Wonderful Counselor

A counselor is someone you go to for advice and help when you are going through hard stuff. If you need to make a really big decision and you have no clue what to do, you can go to a counselor. If your family is having problems, you can all go talk to a counselor. If you feel scared or anxious a lot of the time, a counselor can help you. A counselor is like a life coach, and Jesus is the great life coach—or Wonderful Counselor. He is all for you! He wants you to succeed, and He can help you get there. The Bible has a lot to say about this.

- "I will instruct you and teach you in the way you should go; I will counsel you with my loving eye on you" (Psalm 32:8).

- "You guide me with your counsel, and afterward you will take me into glory" (Psalm 73:24).

- "Trust in the LORD with all your heart and lean not on your own understanding; in all your ways submit to him, and he will make your paths straight" (Proverbs 3:5-6).

We can get super confused if we try to solve our own problems or ask people who might not be helpful—like our friends—for advice. It's not that your friends want to hurt you. It's just that they don't have the wisdom or experience to give you the best advice. And you can always count on Jesus to give you the best advice.

Sometimes even the experts can make mistakes! When I was young and suffered from asthma, my father took me to the doctor to get treatment. But one time, the doctor made a mistake. (Don't worry—this was a long time ago, and you should trust your doctors!) He put the wrong medicine in the syringe. Despite his training and medical wisdom, he gave me the incorrect medicine. Yes, the doctor had gone to school and studied and earned a degree. Yes, the doctor had a license and experience. But the doctor was human. And humans make mistakes.

Jesus, the Wonderful Counselor, never makes a mistake. *Ever.*

Jesus is the Wonderful Counselor because He knows about absolutely everything. He doesn't just have perfect knowledge. He also has perfect understanding. Hebrews 2:17-18 tells us that Jesus became like us so He could better help us. He's felt what you feel. He knows what it's like to be forgotten, overlooked, ignored, and made fun of. He gets it. He gets you. He understands.

> Jesus is the Wonderful Counselor! What questions would you like to ask a counselor about your life? Write them down and then pray and ask for God's help.
>
> _____
>
> _____
>
> _____
>
> _____

Jesus knows where all the roads of life go and where all the detours are, so He can help you get to where you're going. The Bible says there is no information on earth that is beyond what God already knows (Isaiah 46:10). He knows the end from the beginning, down from up, and everything in between.

To get God's help, though, you have to do God's will, be good in His sight, and fear Him. The Bible tells us these things. John 7:17 says, "Anyone who chooses to do the will of God will find out whether my teaching comes from God or whether I speak on my own." That's the doing God's will part. Ecclesiastes 2:26 says, "To the person who pleases him, God gives wisdom, knowledge and happiness." That's the being good in His sight part. Proverbs 1:7 says, "The fear of the LORD is the beginning of knowledge, but fools despise wisdom and instruction." That's the fearing Him part.

Jesus is the Wonderful Counselor, and if you follow His Word, His advice is going to work for you.

Mighty God

When I take my car to a shop to be fixed, it's usually because the car is making some weird noise or a warning light comes on telling me something is wrong. When this happens, I show the mechanic the warning light or tell them about the weird noise. And typically, the mechanic will fix it.

I take my car to the shop because I'm not able to fix it myself. I don't have the knowledge or the tools to do the job right. But the shop does have those things, and they can fix my car so I can continue to drive it without the weird noise or the annoying warning light.

You can go to Jesus for His wonderful counsel and allow Him to determine what is wrong so He can fix what is broken, because He has all the knowledge and tools to pull it off. He can calm your fears and worries. He can help you fix friendships that are a mess. He can give you advice when you have no clue what to do. He can help you in every part of your life.

I have a number of power strips in my house. Power

strips are designed to allow more than two things to be plugged into a single wall outlet. Sometimes two spots just aren't enough. With a power strip, you can connect multiple things—like a computer and a monitor and a printer—at one time.

Life can be like that sometimes. You might feel like you have the strength to handle a problem or two—like a difficult math assignment or a list of chores. But when you add to that getting the flu, having a friend mad at you, and twisting your ankle in gymnastics, you don't have the power to handle everything. That's when you need to plug in to the Mighty God as your power strip. He never runs out of His supply of power, and He has enough power to handle everything you are going through. You just need to be connected to Him.

Do you have any power strips in your house? Look around and notice everything that is plugged into power strips. What are some things in your life—friendships, school, feelings—that you can plug into God's power strip and get His help with?

_____

_____

_____

_____

All through the Bible, we see examples of the power of the Mighty God. One example is how Jesus used His power to overcome sin. He demonstrated His ability to forgive sin. He also healed the sick. Raised the dead. Performed miracles. Everywhere He went, Jesus showed His might and strength.

Eternal Father

The third name for Jesus given to us in Isaiah 9:6 is Eternal Father. This name is probably the one that is least likely to be used by any of us for Jesus. That's because we often call God the Father and Jesus the Son, while forgetting that Jesus is the exact representation of the Father (Hebrews 1:3). Jesus is the reflection of God who came to earth as a man (John 10:30,38). Jesus is not God the Father exactly, but He does have all the character qualities that reflect the Father. In this sense, Jesus is fatherly to us.

This probably sounds confusing, so let me give you an example from my own life. As a pastor and counselor and radio preacher, I often get called Father by people who aren't my actual children. In fact, people who are older than me sometimes call me Father. Now, I'm obviously not replacing their actual fathers in any way. It's just that in some way, they feel like I am like a father to them.

When Isaiah called Jesus by this name, He wanted us to see that Jesus is a Father to us in many ways. He leads us, guides us, gives us good things, encourages us, and protects us. Those are all things a good father does!

As a good Father, Jesus also helps us know how to make the most of our time. It might seem like you have a lot of time right now, but time actually moves very quickly! That's why it's important to use your time in the best way possible—by living your life for Jesus.

Ephesians 5:15-16 says, "Be very careful, then, how you live—not as unwise but as wise, making the most of every opportunity." Jesus is your loving Everlasting Father who wants to see you use your time for the glory of God and the good of others. Like any wise father, He doesn't like to see you waste your time on useless things that aren't going to help you. He wants you to use your time so you experience the best life possible. And He knows exactly how to guide you, instruct you, and motivate you to do just that.

Write down some things you are spending your time on now. Now circle or highlight the things you think are the *best* things to spend your time on. Do you think Jesus would agree?

_____

_____

_____

_____

_____

_____

Prince of Peace

Lastly, Isaiah wants us to know that Jesus is our Prince of Peace. The Hebrew word for peace is "shalom." If you were to visit Israel, you would hear "shalom" used as a form of greeting all the time. But the word "shalom" has a lot more to it than "hi" or "hey." When a Jewish person says "shalom" to you, they aren't just greeting you casually. They are saying they truly hope your life is going great. The word basically means "no more drama," or a peaceful life.

If we were to literally translate this name of Jesus, it might read "Prince of No More Drama." Jesus is the Prince of Calm. He brings us peace.

Now, it's true—life comes with drama. It just does. We can expect ourselves to have bad days, and we can expect other people to have bad days. That's because nobody in this world is perfect, and stuff happens. Yet this name of Jesus is super important because it reminds us that He is the only true source of peace. The Bible says, "I have told you these things, so that in me you may have peace. In this world you will have trouble. But take heart! I have overcome the world" (John 16:33). Jesus has the power to give us peace even on our very worst days.

Have you ever flown in a plane in the middle of a storm? I have. Cups spilled, overhead compartments burst open, and people screamed all around me. I've never been afraid of flying, but in those times, even the calmest among us buckle up and pay attention.

The story is told of a flight that hit some unusual turbulence, tossing the airplane side to side in strong gusts of wind. Clouds looked more like coal. Lightning danced nearby. An eerie silence settled over the passengers in between their shrieks and screams. No one felt safe.

Except for one small child. He sat there with his notebook and pen, drawing a picture of himself climbing a tree on a sunny day. He didn't seem scared at all.

One of the passengers nearby asked the boy, "Aren't you afraid?"

The boy just looked up from his drawing, smiled, and said, "No."

"Why not?" the passenger asked, gripping her seat.

"Because my dad is the pilot," the boy answered calmly before returning to his drawing.

Sometimes life can feel like that airplane ride—scary and wild and seemingly out of control. It's easy to feel afraid. But knowing that Jesus—the Prince of Peace—sits at the controls should make us feel much, much better.

Peace means different things to different people. It might mean no war or no arguing. But the kind of peace that Jesus offers is different from any other kind of peace. His peace gives us calm when we're terrified. When we focus on Him and not on our scary situation, He gives us His peace.

You can't always control what happens to you. You can't control when your friends fight or when your grandma gets sick or when your mom gets a new job and your family needs to move. But you *can* control how you respond to what happens to you. Even better, Jesus can help you control your response. With Jesus, you can let go of the fear you feel.

Have you ever seen an orchestra tuning up for a concert? Maybe you play an instrument in an orchestra or band, and you've experienced this yourself. During this time, everyone is doing their own thing and warming up, and it sounds like chaos. Musical instruments blast out their sounds with no rhyme or reason. But when the conductor walks on stage and raises his baton, his presence changes everything.

Everyone is now focused on him. And then everyone starts to play together, and it sounds really good.

> What does the word "peace" mean to you? Write down everything that comes to mind. As the Prince of Peace, how does Jesus help you?
>
> _____
>
> _____
>
> _____
>
> _____
>
> _____

When you let Jesus into your life as the Prince of Peace, He will put everything in order. What was once a scary storm or chaotic situation calms down. And soon you will discover that all of your life is lining up in order. But that happens only when you agree to trust Him and follow His direction.

In Jesus's names you find counsel, power, direction, peace, and everything else you will ever need. That's why you need to let Jesus guide you in every part of your life. When you talk to Him in prayer and read the Bible and do your best to follow His guidance, His promises will become more than just words—they will become part of your personal experience. And you will sense His love, grace, and peace—and then pass that love, grace, and peace on to everyone you meet.

The name "Sovereign" is yet another name for Jesus. Write down the name here so you can come back to it and remember it later. You can write it fancy or draw some pictures to help you remember it even better.

_____

_____

_____

_____

_____

_____

_____

7

I Am

Jesus is God's selfie. That might sound funny, but it's 100 percent true. A selfie always reflects the image of the person taking the photo, and an image of Jesus is also an image of God.

Jesus is God's selfie because He is the exact representation of God Himself. He isn't just a friend of God. He isn't part of the group hopping into the photo with God. Jesus is the image of God, which makes Him God's selfie.

We can't actually *see* God. And our minds can't understand God. Without Jesus, we can't really know God because God is beyond our understanding. But because He loves us and wanted us to see Him, God got creative and came to us in a form we would be able to understand. He did this by being both man and God at the same time, which is hard to imagine but true!

In John 8:48-59, we come across my favorite name of

Jesus: I Am. When Jesus introduced Himself to the world by this name, He brought some people closer to God—but He also pushed many more away. This is a name you can't believe halfway. Either Jesus is I Am, or He is a liar. That might sound really harsh, but Jesus Himself said so (verses 54-55).

At this point in Jesus's life on earth, He had performed miracles and done things that had given Him a reputation. Some followed Him, and some were really upset by Him. Still others were confused by Him. Was Jesus a good man doing good things? Was He just making things up? Was He...God?

Do you know how it feels to be insulted by someone who doesn't know you? If a kid you don't even know calls you a name, you can just shrug it off. They don't know you at all, so what they said doesn't matter. But what about when someone you know really well, like a friend or teammate, insults you? That's different. That really hurts, doesn't it?

Has anyone ever insulted you or called you a name? How did that make you feel? Do your feelings change depending on who it was that called you the name?

_____

_____

_____

_____

How did Jesus respond when people insulted him—even people He was close to? Maybe He looked away, or maybe

He looked right at the person insulting Him. Maybe He took a deep breath, or maybe He smiled kindly at them. Whatever He did, He answered them, "I honor my Father and you dishonor me" (John 8:49).

The insults kept right on coming. And Jesus kept showing calmness in His responses, not fighting back. I can almost hear His voice softening, like a patient and understanding parent or teacher with a kid who simply won't stop arguing and misbehaving.

Why "I Am"?

So why did Jesus call Himself "I Am"? That seems like a weird name, doesn't it? It's a little complicated, so I'll try to explain. It comes from a Hebrew word that simply means "the four letters." "I Am" is made up of four consonants (you know, the letters that aren't vowels) in the Hebrew language. Originally, the Hebrew language was written without any vowels. And since this name of God had no vowels, it couldn't be pronounced exactly as it was written: YHWH. (Try to say that without vowels. It's impossible!) So YHWH became Yahweh, which became Jehovah, which became LORD.

"I Am" is an important name of Jesus, one that shows His connection to God.

The first word in this name is "I," and "I" is a personal pronoun. This tells us it's the person himself talking. In calling Himself by this name, God is saying He wants to personally talk to us right here, where we live. That's truly amazing!

Not only is the name "I Am" personal, but it's also written in the present tense. "Am" is not past tense ("was"), and it's not future tense ("will be"). Everything about God is *now*. He simply *is*.

Time is different for us than it is for God. We go from one

to ten. That's just how we live because we exist in time and space. But God lives outside time and space. He *is*. The past and the future are like the present to Him.

God is always in the present tense. He's always there for us. That's why we can believe anything He says—because what He declares will happen has already happened in His existence. He's not hoping it will happen. He *knows* it's already happened!

In the Old Testament, when God declared who He was to Moses, He said, "I AM WHO I AM" (Exodus 3:14). He defined Himself by Himself. And this is still true today. We can't make up who we think God is. We can't decide He is something different from who He says He is. He is who He is, and that's the way it is.

"YHWH" ("I Am") is a word without any vowels. Can you think of any other words without any vowels? Write them down—if you can think of any! ("Y" is sometimes used as a vowel, so don't write down words like "my" or "cry.")

_____

_____

_____

The name "I Am" also shows us that God exists as an eternal being who never changes. Hebrews 13:8 says, "Jesus Christ is the same yesterday and today and forever." That's hard to imagine, isn't it? People change. We all change. We grow and change physically. We change inside. Maybe your favorite color was green, but now it's blue. Maybe you used to be short, but you had a growth spurt, and now you're tall. Maybe you used to be shy, but now you're very talkative.

But Jesus never changes. Just as water is wet, the sun is hot, and the sky is blue by their very nature, Jesus's nature is forever unchanged.

God Never Changes

James 1:17 says, "Every good and perfect gift is from above, coming down from the Father of the heavenly lights, who does not change like shifting shadows." God does not change. He might change His mind or change His approach as He works with us, but that has to do with our relationship with Him.

This might be getting a little confusing, so let me give you an example. The sun does not change. It is planet Earth that rotates around the sun. Half the earth is dark at any given time, not because the sun changes but because the earth's relationship to the sun changes. Seasons change. Weather patterns change. But none of that happens because the sun has changed. It all happens because of the earth's rotation and its orbit around the sun. It is the earth that has adjusted, not the sun.

When we are like the earth and adjust to God (who is like the sun) or move in relation to Him, it may seem like God has changed because the results of our relationship with Him change, but He Himself has not changed. We're just seeing a different part of Him because our view has changed.

Seven times in the book of John, Jesus referred to Himself as "I Am."

- "I am the bread of life. Whoever comes to me will

never go hungry, and whoever believes in me will never be thirsty" (6:35).

- "I am the light of the world. Whoever follows me will never walk in the darkness, but will have the light of life" (8:12).

- "Very truly I tell you, I am the gate for the sheep" (10:7).

- "I am the good shepherd. The good shepherd lays down his life for the sheep...I am the good shepherd; I know my sheep and my sheep know me" (10:11,14).

- "I am the resurrection and the life. The one who believes in me will live, even though they die" (11:25).

- "I am the way and the truth and the life. No one comes to the Father except through me" (14:6).

- "I am the true vine, and my Father is the gardener...I am the vine; you are the branches. If you remain in me and I in you, you will bear much fruit; apart from me you can do nothing" (15:1,5).

Let's look at each of these verses individually to understand more about the name "I Am."

I Am the Bread of Life

When Jesus said He is the bread of life and that He is able to satisfy our hunger and our thirst, He was letting us know that He is all we need spiritually. Just as your body gets hungry, so does your soul. When you know Jesus personally and trust in Him, you no longer are hungry on the inside.

Do you know what it's like to have hot bread come out

of the oven when you are hungry, and you get some butter and jam to put on it? You probably start drooling before you even bite into it! This bread satisfies you deeply. In the same way, Jesus can satisfy your heart and soul when you make Him a part of your life.

I Am the Light of the World

Jesus not only feeds you but also lights your way. When you follow Him, He will allow you to see where you're going. When you walk with Him, He gives you light. He shows you where you're going and helps you make good choices. With Him lighting your way, you can see where you need to go, and you won't stumble or get lost.

I Am the Door of the Sheep

To understand this description, you need a little background. Every shepherd has a gate. This is a door through which the sheep can enter. John 10:9 says, "I am the gate; whoever enters through me will be saved. They will come in and go out, and find pasture." This door gives us entrance into heaven—but it also gives us more! This verse says we can go in and out, and that through Jesus, we can discover good pasture here on earth.

Verse 10 tells us even more. "The thief comes only to steal and kill and destroy; I have come that they may have life, and have it to the full." Jesus lived and died and rose again so that we could have eternal life in heaven and the *best* kind of life now.

I Am the Good Shepherd

A shepherd not only opens the door for the sheep to enter but also watches over his sheep. He is responsible for them. If anything happens to the sheep, the shepherd gets the blame—not the sheep. This is because sheep depend completely on the shepherd.

As the great I Am, Jesus has your back directionally, spiritually, emotionally, physically, and eternally. He knows exactly what you need and when you need it. When Jesus is your shepherd, He will lead you where you need to go.

I Am the Resurrection and the Life

Jesus came that He might give life, but He also came as the life itself. He is the power of the resurrection, and He is life. When you allow your problems to draw you to Him, He will calm you in the middle of chaos. He promises to comfort you when you are afraid or anxious.

I Am the Way and the Truth and the Life

In John 14:6, Jesus didn't just tell us that He knows the way. He told us that He *is* the way. When we put our trust in Him, He takes us where we need to go. He opens doors we couldn't even knock on. He is the way, and He makes things better for us in every way.

And Jesus is also the truth. He's not *a* truth; He's *the* truth. Everything Jesus says is true, and all truth comes from Him. No one can decide that one plus one equals eleven just because they want it to. It will never equal eleven, no matter what. Truth is truth.

Jesus is the standard, and He has spoken. If you choose to live any way other than His way, you will not have life. The only way to get the life He offers—the abundant life, or life "to the full"—is to follow His path according to His truth.

I Am the True Vine

Jesus is the real deal. There's nothing fake about Him. He's the original. And in order to access His power, you need to follow Him. Strangely enough, it's when you *rest* in Jesus that He does His work in you and through you.

It's super common today for people to live just for themselves and care only about themselves. They make life all about them. But that's not how it works. Jesus is the vine, and He supplies life to the fruit, so when you stay connected to Him (the vine), your life will produce the best kind of fruit. It will be sweet and tasty, not nasty and rotten. But you can produce good fruit—like being kind to others and being patient and loving—only if you stay connected to the vine, Jesus.

Think of some ways you have changed in the past year or two—or even five! Write them down. God *never* changes, and you can always count on Him to be exactly who He says He is!

_____

_____

_____

He Is Everything You Need

When you stay connected to Jesus, you will discover the plans He has for you—plans that will absolutely amaze you! You will also discover the power He has for you to carry out those plans.

You can always trust Jesus.

I don't know what you're struggling with or what makes you sad or what you are praying for. But I do know this:

When you know the great I Am, you always have help, no matter what's happening in your life. There is so much power in Jesus's name!

Jesus is the I Am. And "I Am" means that He is everything you need. He is whatever you are missing. He is whatever you need Him to be. When you get to know Him more, seek Him more, and connect yourself with Him more, you can live the best life ever!

What are the seven different aspects of the great I Am that you learned in this chapter?

1. I Am the _____.

2. I Am the _____.

3. I Am the _____.

4. I Am the _____.

5. I Am the _____.

6. I Am the _____.

7. I Am the _____.

The name "I Am" is yet another name for Jesus. Write down the name here so you can come back to it and remember it later. You can write it fancy or draw some pictures to help you remember it even better.

8

Lord

Have you ever been watching TV when suddenly the words "no signal" appeared on your screen? That's what happens to many believers who don't know this next name of Jesus we're going to explore.

A lot of times, people think the name Lord is just something to throw into their prayers to make them sound better. Or something to say in Sunday school. But this name is actually super important. It carries authority.

It's easy to confuse the terms "power" and "authority." Satan has power. He dominates the world we live in and influences people's lives in many ways. His actions are both real and damaging. But what he doesn't have is final authority. Authority is the right to use the power you possess.

For example, football players are almost always bigger and stronger and faster than the referees. The players can knock people down. That's power. But the referees make the final call on a play and can even put someone out of a game. That's authority.

Satan has power, but he can use that power over you only if you don't follow Jesus as Lord.

How can a person be in two places at once? (Hint: It involves technology!) Think about a time when you were in two places at once. How did you do this?

_____

_____

_____

Two Kingdoms

Colossians 1:13 tells us that God has "rescued us from the dominion of darkness and brought us into the kingdom of the Son he loves." By rescuing us, He allowed us to live our lives under the rule of a new King, the Lord Jesus Christ. When you follow Jesus as Lord in your home, at school, and out in the world, you stay connected to Him, and nothing can break that connection.

If you are a believer in Jesus Christ, then when He died, you died with Him. When Christ rose, you rose with Him. When Christ was seated at the right hand of the Father, you were seated with Him. You were made to live life along with Jesus.

Since Jesus is seated at the right hand of God (the "power side"), His followers are seated there with Him (Ephesians 2:6). You might be wondering how someone can be in two places at once. Easy—we do it all the time through technology! I can physically be in Dallas, but I can also be in Chicago through Skype. I can be hanging out at home and still participate in a Zoom meeting in Atlanta. Through technology, we can be in two places at once.

If people can produce technology that lets us be in two places at once, don't you think that God could do the same thing? You are living physically on earth, but you are also spiritually connected to God's kingdom in heaven. You have two homes—heaven and earth—and God is your ruler in both homes.

> When you become a Christian and Jesus becomes Lord of your life, it should affect everything you do. Are there any parts of your life that you can let Jesus help you with right now?
>
> _____
>
> _____
>
> _____

Experiencing God's Kingdom

If you're not totally sure that you are experiencing God's kingdom rule in your life, you can make sure of it today. Here's how:

> "The word is near you; it is in your mouth and in your heart," that is, the message concerning faith that we proclaim: If you declare with your mouth,

"Jesus is Lord," and believe in your heart that God raised him from the dead, you will be saved. For it is with your heart that you believe and are justified, and it is with your mouth that you profess your faith and are saved. As Scripture says, "Anyone who believes in him will never be put to shame." For there is no difference between Jew and Gentile—the same Lord is Lord of all and richly blesses all who call on him, for, "Everyone who calls on the name of the Lord will be saved" (Romans 10:8-13).

If you want to experience the presence and power of Jesus and His kingdom authority, you need to do two things. First, you must believe in your heart that Jesus died and rose again for your personal salvation, which saves you for heaven. And second, you must publicly declare with your mouth and your life that Jesus is Lord. This confession brings you victory on earth.

When you say Jesus is your Lord, it should affect everything you do. As Colossians 3:17 says, "Whatever you do, whether in word or deed, do all in the name of the Lord Jesus, giving thanks to God the Father through him."

When the New Testament was being written, people were often punished or persecuted if they declared Jesus as Lord. Today, in our culture, that doesn't happen so much. But sometimes people are embarrassed to say they think Jesus is Lord, or they're not sure how someone will react when they talk about Jesus. But we can't skip this part of following God.

When you become a Christian, you might choose to wear a cross necklace or carry your Bible with you or post your favorite verses on social media. But having Jesus as Lord of your life means more than that. It means He rules. He chooses. His truth is the truth you go by. What He says and what He does totally affect what you say and what you do. Jesus influences your life at school, at home, and anywhere else you go.

> What are some of your favorite brands—clothes, technology, even stuff like water bottles or pens? Remember, Jesus isn't just a brand. He is Lord!
>
> _____
>
> _____
>
> _____

Jesus isn't a decoration. He's not a logo or a brand. He is Lord. Ruler. Master. King. The authority over all (Ephesians 1:22).

For some Christians, Jesus is important, but He's not the main thing. He gets some of their attention as they attend church, pray before they eat, read a Bible verse in the morning, or decorate their laptop cover or phone case with some Jesus stickers. But when it comes to choosing between Jesus (what He says, where He leads, what He requires) and the other stuff in their lives (personal, emotional, and physical; friends, media, and so on), Jesus sometimes loses.

And when Jesus loses—when people choose other things instead of Him—they lose.

They lose because Jesus is our access to all we need so we can live our lives with the maximum power we can have, and we can get that power only through Jesus.

Calling on the Lord

Nothing exists or happens without Jesus. The Bible makes that clear:

> The Son is the image of the invisible God, the first-born over all creation. For in him all things were created: things in heaven and on earth, visible and invisible, whether thrones or powers or rulers or authorities; all things have been created through him and for him. He is before all things, and in him all things hold together. And he is the head of the body, the church; he is the beginning and the first-born from among the dead, so that in everything he might have the supremacy (Colossians 1:15-18).

Jesus is Lord over our entire world! Write down what this means to you.

_____

_____

_____

Jesus should be involved in all parts of your life. Every subject in school. Every friendship you have. Every sport or activity or hobby you like to do. Every relationship you have—from your parents to your teachers to your siblings to people you meet just once. Everything you do that's fun (like sleepovers and birthday parties) and everything you do that's not so fun (like chores and homework).

Jesus wants you to call on Him when you need His help, and He wants you to talk to Him when everything is going great. He wants to be a part of all the things you say, the decisions you make, the reasons you make them, the thoughts you think, and the activities you participate in. You need to live every part of your life with Jesus as Lord of it.

God doesn't just want you to declare that Jesus exists. He wants you to declare that Jesus is Lord. Why? Because it brings Him glory. And He totally deserves all the glory we can give Him!

Jesus is Lord over all. He is over you. He is over me. He is over our entire world!

"Lord" is yet another name for Jesus. Write down the name here so you can come back to it and remember it later. You can write it fancy or draw some pictures to help you remember it even better.

_____

_____

_____

9

Jesus

John. Jacob. Noah. Michael. Elizabeth. Grace. Hannah. Victoria. These are some of the most common names in America. You have probably met people with these names. For whatever reason, parents frequently choose to name their kids these names. They might like what the name means. Or they might have had relatives or ancestors with those names. Whatever the case, these names tend to get passed down more often than most.

Just like the name Jesus.

Not so much today, but at the time Jesus was born more than 2,000 years ago, "Jesus" was a popular name.

Jesus was not named by His parents. We discover in the Bible that heaven sent a message to Joseph through an angel and told him to name the baby Jesus (see Matthew 1:18-25).

This common name would eventually become His most well-known name. Jesus means "Savior," "rescuer," and "deliverer." The Old Testament name for Jesus was Joshua.

You might remember that Joshua was the man who delivered the Israelites into the Promised Land and overcame Israel's enemies. He was fierce and full of faith. The name Joshua (or Jesus in Greek) means someone who leads the way into a place of blessing.

God chose a name for His Son that means "Savior." Matthew 1:21 says it clearly: "[Mary] will give birth to a son, and you are to give him the name Jesus, because he will save his people from their sins."

What are some of the most popular names you can think of? Now ask your parents and/or grandparents what the popular names were when they were kids. Are any of these names the same?

_____

_____

_____

Rescue!

When I was a water safety instructor and lifeguard, my main job was to rescue people from drowning. Sure, I had other responsibilities, like teaching people how to swim, helping people become better swimmers, and just helping out at the pool. But those tasks were secondary to my main objective: to save lives and rescue people from drowning. If I hadn't been able to do that, I wouldn't have been able to be a lifeguard. Saving lives was the main part of my job.

People often want to use Jesus for everything except His main job. They want Jesus to rescue them from sickness, from poverty, from problems with their friends, from getting bad grades, or from feeling sad all the time. And while Jesus *can* and *will* help us with all of these things, His main job is rescuing us from our sins.

What happens when you skin your knee? How do you take care of the problem? How does God deal with the problem of sin and clean things up?

_____

_____

_____

Jesus came to save us and give us eternal life, but He also came that we might have the best life here on earth (John 10:10).

Have you ever prayed for something but it didn't happen? That's because sometimes we skip over Jesus's main job—saving us to give us eternal life *and* the best life here on earth—and we try to use Him like a vending machine instead. We tell Him what we want instead of asking Him what He wants for us (which is always what is best!).

The Problem with Sin

Did you know that all the bad things in your life, like being selfish or jealous, have to do with sin? They're the result of either your own sin or someone else's sin. In this world there is always going to be sin. And that's going to mess everything up. Always. You know how millions of people in America got sick with COVID-19? That's how sin is—it spreads like a coronavirus. And sin infects all of us because all of us sin.

To understand how Jesus deals with sin, we need to understand some things about God. For starters, God is perfect. Everything about Him is perfect. He is flawless. He has no issues and makes no mistakes. And He notices all sin because He is pure.

Have you ever fallen off your bike and skinned your knee? Your mom or dad didn't automatically put medication on the open wound, did they? No, first they had to wash the dirt off the wound and possibly even pick out some gravel. Any amount of dirt or gravel, no matter how tiny, could cause infection down the road. Your skinned knee needed to be cleaned before the medication could fully work.

Everything about God is perfect, and He cannot and will not allow even the slightest speck of dirt or gravel—or sin—to enter into His presence. That's why Jesus is God's representative to deal with the yuckiness of our sin. Through the cleansing power of His blood, we discover the cure to any problem. Because if you don't deal with the cause of the problem—which is sin—the problem will only get worse.

Kinds of Sin

Just as there are many kinds of bacteria in the world, there are also many kinds of sin. We have all sinned, yes. But these sins are as varied as the snowflakes in a storm. Whether it's something you do on purpose (like deliberately telling a lie) or doing one thing when you should have done something else, all sin results in death.

People sin in a lot of ways, and there are three main categories of sin: imputed, inherited, and personal.

Imputed sin is the sin that comes directly from Adam, the very first man. Basically, because Adam sinned, all of us are sinners. We have no chance of being perfect. This might not sound fair, but it's true. Ever since Adam, nobody has lived a perfect life without any sin (except Jesus). Yes, there are some really nice people who don't ever seem to do anything wrong, but even those people have sinned. It's impossible to never, ever sin!

Inherited sin is what we receive from our parents and ancestors. We know this as our "sin nature." Every person ever born (again, except for Jesus) has a sin nature. That's why a parent never has to teach a child how to be selfish, how to be sneaky, or how to lie. A parent *does* have to teach a child how to share, how to love, and how to be patient. Because sin is inherited, we all sin.

Personal sin is the sin we know we shouldn't do, but we go ahead and do it anyway. Or it's the right action we know we should take—like standing up for someone who is being picked on or helping our sister with the dishes—but we choose not to. We all sin in this way, and God can see our heart (even if nobody else can), so He can see this type of sin.

Good News!

Don't worry though! There's good news in this "bad news" chapter! John 11:26 tells us this good news: "Whoever lives by believing in me will never die."

It's hard to imagine, but we shouldn't be afraid of death. If you believe in Jesus, you won't even know you died. You will immediately be with Him in heaven. Jesus has saved us from death, and He's also saved us from the power of sin and its ability to mess up our lives here on earth.

Write down the three kinds of sin you learned about in this chapter. Can you give an example of each kind? (Bonus: Use examples from your own life and experiences!)

_____

_____

_____

Because of Jesus, you can deal with anything sin throws your way. You can do this when you use the name of Jesus. Of course, you can't just say "Jesus" and expect everything to go perfectly. Most of us end our prayers by saying, "In Jesus's name," because that's what we've been taught to pray. But that's not going to automatically give us everything we want.

Jesus's name is not a magic word, like "hocus-pocus." It doesn't come infused with superhero powers. Rather, Jesus's name gives you access to a power greater than any magic or superhero powers ever could—especially when you are closely following Him.

The Bible says, "This is the confidence we have in approaching God: that if we ask anything according to his will, he hears us. And if we know that he hears us—whatever we ask—we know that we have what we asked of him" (1 John 5:14-15). The important words here are "according to his will." God is not going to respond to your use of Jesus's name if you are not planning to do His will.

John 15:7 says, "If you remain in me and my words remain in you, ask whatever you wish, and it will be done for you." And John 14:13-15 says, "I will do whatever you ask in my name, so that the Father may be glorified in the Son. You may ask me for anything in my name, and I will do it. If you love me, keep my commands."

Loving Jesus means keeping His commands. Remaining in Jesus means having the truth of His Word—His viewpoint on every decision you make—influence everything you do. When these two things take place, you are guaranteed to receive whatever you ask. Because when you do these two things, you are in His will, and whatever it is you are asking, He wants as well.

Think of a time when sin messed up your life. What happened? How could God have helped you—or someone else—make a better choice?

_____

_____

_____

Jesus may have been a common name back when He was born, but because of what He did and who He is, this name has never been the same since. And it will never be the same in the future either. In fact, in the future, regardless of how powerful people are, every knee will bow to the name of Jesus, and every tongue will acknowledge that Jesus is Lord.

Who is your favorite superhero? What powers does he or she have? Jesus has more power than any superhero, and through His name, you have access to that power!

_____

_____

_____

The name Jesus is yet another name for...yep—Jesus! Write down the name here so you can come back to it and remember it later. You can write it fancy or draw some pictures to help you remember it even better.

_____

_____

_____

_____

10

Christ

My given name is Anthony Tyrone Evans. That's the name my parents chose for me when I was born. Most people, though, know me as Tony Evans. When I hear people say that name, I turn around to respond. And when I'm with my family at home, I'm called Poppy (by my grandkids) or Daddy (by my kids). If I'm with my family and someone says "Anthony," I won't look up, because that is the name my son goes by.

I'm also known as Dr. Evans and Pastor. As you can see, people refer to me in a lot of ways! They can separate out names, like Tony, Doc, or Pastor. Or they can combine names, like Dr. Tony Evans. But no matter what name someone uses, people are still talking about me when they say any of my names.

Same with Jesus. We find a variety of names by which Jesus is called throughout Scripture. When the names King of kings and Lord of lords are used together, He is known as the Lord Jesus Christ. At times we just read about Jesus. At other times, He's simply known as Lord or Christ. All the Bible writers were speaking about the same person, but each name has its own special meaning.

What are the different names you go by? Who calls you what name?

_____

_____

_____

Jesus's various names aren't random. They aren't just fun nicknames. Each one has a specific meaning, and each one tells you more about Him. For example, Tony Evans is my personal identity, Doctor is my title, Pastor is my role or responsibility, and Poppy is what my grandchildren call me. "Jesus" is our Lord's personal identity. That name shows His ability to rescue us—mostly from sin but also from sickness, hunger, loneliness, and more.

Besides the name Jesus, we also know Him as Christ. Now, Christ is not Jesus's last name. It is His role or position. The word "Christ" is seen more than 500 times in the New Testament, and it also means "Messiah." "Messiah" literally means "the anointed one," or the one chosen by God for a specific purpose and given the power to carry out that purpose.

The entire Old Testament talks about the coming of the Messiah. That's because Jesus is the Christ, the anointed one from God who fulfills the promises God gave to the world.

All About Family

The Bible predicted that Christ would come through the lineage—or family line—of King David.

Now, I know that reading a bunch of hard-to-pronounce names in the Bible is probably not your favorite thing to do—nor is it mine. It can be pretty boring, actually. But those names are important because they prove that Jesus is the Son of God.

History shows us that when God connected Mary and Joseph, He connected two people who both descended from King David. God's actions always have meaning.

When the Bible talks about "the anointed one," it is talking about a person who was chosen—or elected—for a certain position, like when someone is elected to an office (such as a president or mayor).

In biblical days, God chose some people to serve as *prophets* to speak on His behalf. He chose other people to serve as *priests* to stand between God and the people by presenting sacrifices for the forgiveness of sins. And He chose some to serve as *kings* to rule over nations.

Christ, the Messiah, combined all three positions—prophet, priest, and king—into one.

Prophet

As a prophet, every time Jesus spoke, He spoke with God's authority. After all, He is God, so this makes perfect sense. John 1:1 says, "In the beginning was the Word, and the Word was with God, and the Word was God." When Jesus spoke, God was actually the one doing the talking.

Jesus Christ is the last word on any and every subject. He has the final say-so on everything. You name the subject, and whatever it is, Jesus has the final word on it.

If we mix any other words or ideas with Christ's words, we are not getting the truth of His Word. It's like adding a teaspoon of poison to a pot of soup. The entire soup is ruined. Christ is the beginning and the end of all truth. We can save ourselves a lot of confusion and frustration in life if we always ask ourselves one simple question: What did Jesus say?

Priest

Do you know what a mediator is? A mediator is basically a go-between. If you're in a fight with a friend and another friend helps both of you make up and become friends again, that person is a mediator. A priest is kind of like that. The priest goes between the people and God to help make things right.

Now, a lot of people talk about God but leave out Jesus, or Christ. Jesus is the One who gives us access to God. If you skip Jesus, you lose access to God. Jesus is the go-between who lets sinful people—all of us—connect to a holy God.

Christ is a priest who understands how we feel. God the Father knows everything, but He has not felt everything because He hasn't lived on this earth like Christ has.

That's why God sent His Son to earth as a man. Jesus understands loneliness. He knows what pain feels like. He gets rejection and being left out or made fun of. He even experienced death—both the death of those He loved and His own death. In fact, there's no part of life that Jesus hasn't experienced.

King

In the Bible, we read about King David being anointed as the ruler over Israel. But now that Christ has come, He is the ruler and King over all. Revelation 11:15 says,

The seventh angel sounded his trumpet, and there were loud voices in heaven, which said:

"The kingdom of the world has become
the kingdom of our Lord and of his Messiah;
and he will reign for ever and ever."

A lot of people say that Christ is their King, but they don't act like it. Their actions say, "He may be the King, but He's not the King over me." If you don't allow Christ to influence the choices you make about what you do, how you treat people, what you do with your time, the way you respond to good and bad things that happen to you, and everything else in your life, then you aren't allowing Him to be King of your life.

If we know Christ personally, He is in charge of our lives. We act the way He wants us to act. We say the things He wants us to say. We make the choices He wants us to make.

You can experience the best life Christ has for you when you allow Him to be your prophet, priest, and King.

What are the three positions that Christ combined into one? Write down a little bit about each one.

_____

_____

_____

Living for Christ

My favorite verse in the Bible explains how we experience the goodness of Christ.

I have been crucified with Christ and I no longer live, but Christ lives in me. The life I now live in the body, I live by faith in the Son of God, who loved me and gave himself for me (Galatians 2:20).

The closer you draw to Christ and the more you allow His words to become your own, the more you will live the life He intended you to live. You will have joy and peace, and others will see that in you and want to know more.

If you've watched track and field events, you've seen high jumpers use their legs to jump as high as they can and clear a bar. Great high jumpers can get higher than seven feet—which is pretty high when you think about it.

Think of some ways you can make Christ more a part of your life—how you treat people, what you do with your time, which choices you make. What can you change to make Him more a part of these things?

_____

_____

_____

There's a similar event called the pole vault. Pole vaulters sprint with a long pole in their hands, and then they stick the pole in the ground in order to clear a much higher bar. Pole vaulters can jump well over twice as high as any high jumper. Some have even gone over 19 feet!

Now, a high jumper and a pole vaulter are trying to do the same thing. They are trying to get over a bar. But one uses only their own body. The other is using something else to propel them farther than they could go on their own—and they go so much higher.

You may be able to get so far on your own without leaning on God. But it won't be very far. When you rely on Christ—when you grab the pole of the Prophet, Priest, and King—you can do more than you ever even dreamed. You can love people you never even liked. You can be kind when you would normally be unkind. You can say nice words instead of mean ones. You can stay calm when you would normally lose it. You can make good decisions instead of making bad decisions or no decision at all.

What does "the goodness" of Christ mean to you? Write down Galatians 2:20 and then write down what it means in your own words.

_____

_____

_____

_____

When Christ works in you and through you, you will be able to go above and beyond what you ever imagined you could do. Placing your faith in Jesus gives you the power to go higher than you ever dreamed.

"Christ" is yet another name for Jesus. Write down the name here so you can come back to it and remember it later. You can write it fancy or draw some pictures to help you remember it even better.

_____

_____

_____

_____

_____

11

Son of God, Son of Man

J esus is both the Son of God and the Son of Man. How could He be two Sons at once? And how did this happen?

Jesus shows us God's heart, His goals, His character, His attributes, and His desires (John 14:7-11; Hebrews 1:1-3). But He also identifies with our heart, our goals, our character, our attributes, and our desires. He can do this because He is both fully God (the Son of God) and fully human (the Son of Man). This is why He could be hungry one moment and feed 5,000 people then next. He could be thirsty one moment and walk on water the next. One moment He died, and the next moment He rose from the dead. He is both the Son of God and the Son of Man.

Did you know that everything that is true about God—grace, mercy, justice, and so on—is also true about Jesus? God and Jesus share all of those amazing characteristics!

Yet not only is Jesus the Son of God—He is also the Son of Man. As the Son of Man walking around here on earth, Jesus got tired and hungry. He had a favorite food. He needed sleep. He cried when He was sad. He was even tempted by the devil. Everything that makes us human, Jesus experienced—except for sin.

Write down some normal, ordinary things you do every day, like eat breakfast, take a shower, and play with your friends. Which of these things do you think Jesus did when He lived on earth?

_____

_____

_____

_____

_____

More Than About You

Most of us believe that Jesus came to earth to take us to heaven. And while that's true, it's not the end of the story.

Jesus came to do much more than that. Yes, He did come so that you would have a way to heaven, but He also died and rose again to bring heaven (its rule, authority, power, grace, confidence, compassion, wisdom, and more) to you on earth. With Jesus, you can have all these things! Jesus also came so that Satan won't rule you anymore. This is very good news!

Did you know that God has given you a very specific purpose that only you can fulfill? That purpose is super important. A lot of believers don't live out their specific purpose because they don't realize they can!

Your life was never meant to be only about you.

God wants you to use your time, talents, and treasures for His glory and for the good of other people. Just as Jesus had two purposes as the Son of God and as the Son of Man, once you become a follower of God, you also have two purposes. You are to set your thoughts on things above (Colossians 3:2)—preparing and planning for rewards in heaven—while also doing what God wants you to do here on earth (Matthew 6:10).

What are some of your talents? (Think about what you like to do and what you are naturally pretty good at.) How can you use your talents to bless others?

_____

_____

_____

_____

_____

When you accept Jesus, He gives you power over sin. And since Jesus can know no sin, He can show you how to be the person you were created to be. He can help you obey your parents and teachers. He can remind you of happy things when you're feeling sad. He can help you speak up when you see someone being bullied—and He can even help you show kindness to the bully. Jesus can do anything!

When Jesus lived on earth, He and God remained so familiar with each other that Jesus called God "Father." Jesus chose to call God that family-oriented name time and time again. Many of us have not discovered more of God's presence in our lives because we only know Him as God. He has not yet become Father, or Daddy. But the longer you walk with Him and the better you get to know Him, the more you will see Him as an amazing Father!

What are some things you would like Jesus to help you with? Write them down here—and then pray about them!

_____

_____

_____

_____

Through Jesus, we have been adopted by God so that He is legally our Father. As we get to know Jesus better and better and let God work in our lives, we'll become more and more like Jesus, and it will become more and more obvious that we're children of God (Romans 8:28-29).

Greater Things

As the Son of God and the Son of Man, Jesus knows everything and understands everything. That's why He can give you all you need in your life on earth—and He can also lead you to heaven to live with Him someday!

You might still be wondering about the power of Jesus that you read about, sing about, and hear about in church. You want to see God for yourself. You don't want Him to be far away. You want Him to be right here with you. And God *will* be right here with you—He will even send His angels to you (Hebrews 1:14)—but only when you first honor and acknowledge Jesus as God. As the Son of God, Jesus is the exact reflection of God Himself.

When you stay close to God, you get to experience greater things than you could ever imagine. But if you choose not to follow Jesus in your daily life, you will never be able to experience all the wonderful things He can do for you, and you'll miss out on so much great stuff. It comes down to obedience and faith, and it's totally your choice.

If you decide to follow Jesus and do as He says, amazing things will happen in your life! Jesus is both the Son of God and the Son of Man, connecting heaven with earth and giving you all you need to live out your unique purpose. You'll live for God and live for others—and there's no better way to live your life!

"Son of God" and "Son of Man" are yet two more names for Jesus. Write down those names here so you can come back to them and remember them later. You can write them fancy or draw some pictures to help you remember them even better.

_____

_____

_____

_____

_____

12

Word of God

Where did everything come from?

Some people believe that the earth was formed like this: At the very beginning there was *nothing*. But then, following a sudden big bang, there was *something*. After that, over the process of billions of years, the earth evolved into everything we see today, including you and me.

I think it takes a lot of faith to believe in a scenario like that, especially since there isn't really any solid evidence behind the story. In fact, I think it takes more faith to believe in evolution than to believe the creation story the Bible tells.

Evolution suggests that God isn't necessary. That He doesn't matter. However, when we remove God from the story, we are left without meaning and purpose.

The Bible tells a different story.

How do you imagine the earth being made? You can write a story or draw a picture.

_____

_____

_____

_____

_____

_____

_____

Word = God

John 1:1 reminds us that Jesus was there at the very first moment of creation: "In the beginning was the Word, and the Word was with God, and the Word was God." Jesus is right there on page one of history. Though He doesn't show up in human form until the start of the New Testament, He's been on the scene since before the curtains ever opened.

The last of Jesus's names we're going to get to know is "Word of God." In the Bible, we learn that the Word was the start of all things. In fact, He existed before the start of all things. We know this because John 1:1 uses the past tense *was* and not the present tense *is* when introducing the Word. The Word was there before the beginning, and the Word existed before everything else.

This might all sound like some crazy time-travel story, but it's true.

The Bible also tells us that "the Word was *with* God." The word "with" here means "face-to-face." You know how it is when you're having a really great conversation with your mom or best friend, and you're looking at each other and laughing or crying or just having a really good talk? It's like that between God and Jesus—all the time!

The Bible also tells us that the Word *was* God. God is the only one who does not need anything outside Himself in order to be Himself. Think of a really simple math concept, like 1 = 1. Word = God.

Finally, the Bible tells us that the Word became flesh. This might sound kind of strange, but it's what happened when Jesus came to earth. He lived as a human here on earth, just like each of us does.

"Word" can take on many meanings, especially when it has to do with communication—like when someone says, "I'd like to have a word with you." When we speak a word with someone or to someone, we are saying things to them. In that same way, the Word is the way we can talk to God.

Whenever we see the name "Word" in the Bible, it means both the message of God and a person. The Word is more than what we read. It's also who Jesus is. Remember, Word = God.

God's Word is equal to God's person because the Word was God. The Word *is* God.

When we don't believe in the Word—who is God—we think we can make up our own truth, run things the way we want, and answer to no one at all. But if we want to run our own world, we should go make our own world, because God made this one, and He calls the shots.

> Write down a few sentences with "word" in them. Do you see how "word" can have several meanings?
>
> _____
>
> _____
>
> _____
>
> _____

Here's what God says about the creation of this world:

> For in him all things were created: things in heaven and on earth, visible and invisible, whether thrones or powers or rulers or authorities; all things have been created through him and for him. He is before all things, and in him all things hold together (Colossians 1:16-17).

The world was made by God through Jesus and for Jesus. It wasn't made just for us. Jesus is the reason God made it in the first place. The Bible tells us that all things were created "through him and for him." When God created the world through Jesus, He gave it to Jesus as a present. Believing this helps us find peace, faith, and purpose.

Life and Light

Genesis 1:1-3 says, "In the beginning God created the heavens and the earth. Now the earth was formless and empty, darkness was over the surface of the deep, and the Spirit of God was hovering over the waters. And God said, 'Let there be light,' and there was light." The word "light" here means "life."

John 1:4-5 says, "In him was life, and that life was the light of all mankind. The light shines in the darkness, and the darkness has not overcome it." Jesus is the light—the life—that God spoke into creation.

As you get to know Jesus as the Word, you come face-to-face with all the ways He gives you life and light. We don't often think of Jesus in this way, as the Creator of living plants, living animals, living people, and the entire cycle of life itself. We imagine God creating and running everything for Himself, and then Jesus showing up centuries later. But the name "Word" tells us something different. Jesus was not only an active participant in the creation process but also the very reason creation was made. He is the giver and receiver of life.

In Jesus we are given the light we need to live, because His life is "the light of all mankind" (John 1:4).

What does light do? It allows us to see. So in Jesus, we can see. But it might be easier to understand this idea if we say the opposite: Without Jesus, there is no light, and we live in darkness.

When someone rejects Jesus as the one who created everything and the one for whom everything was created, that person walks in darkness. Rejecting Jesus means rejecting light and living in darkness. When Jesus's way of looking at things is not your way of looking at things, you have rejected Him. When Jesus's decisions are not your decisions, you have rejected Him. When Jesus's love is not allowed to flow from your heart to others, you have rejected Him. And to reject Jesus is to turn off the light and stumble around in the darkness.

Light always overcomes darkness. Always. No matter how dark it is or how long it has been dark, when you light a candle or turn on a lamp, everything changes. Darkness always leaves when you turn on the light.

Look around at all the different ways light comes into your house. (It could be natural light that comes in through the windows or light from lamps or even candlelight.) How does Jesus give you light in your life?

_____

_____

_____

_____

Bottom line: It's all about Jesus. And when you choose not to make your life all about Jesus, you are on your own. That's why the Bible tells us, "Whether you eat or drink or whatever you do, do it all for the glory of God (1 Corinthians 10:31). Even when we're doing something as everyday and boring as eating cereal or drinking water, we can do it for God's glory.

The secret to life is simply to give more and more glory back to Jesus. Because when you do, He will put more and more life into you and whatever it is you are doing. See, the name "Word" isn't merely a word. This name represents the entire reason you exist. Jesus, the Word, is to be the center of your life. He is the giver of life and the purpose of life itself.

Jesus Is One of a Kind!

We read in John 1:14 that Jesus took on flesh—or became human—and "dwelt among us." Jesus came into a sinful world, bringing life where life was not found. And He still brings life to us today.

What are some things that make your life brighter (pets, books, music, sports, friends...)? How does Jesus make these things—and your life—even brighter?

_____

_____

_____

_____

Jesus walked the streets in Israel. He talked. He ate. He laughed. He cried. He hung out with His friends. He did all the things humans do, but He did them as the Word—the messenger of God. John 1:14 says that we "have seen his glory, the glory of the one and only Son, who came from the Father." "One and only" means that Jesus is one of a kind. There is nobody else like Him. There never has been another Jesus, nor will there ever be.

If you live in the light of Jesus and follow His written Word (the Bible) and His guidance, you will experience the best kind of life possible. From the very beginning, Jesus has been the life and light of this world and of your life.

"Word" is yet another name for Jesus. Write down this name here so you can come back to it and remember it later. You can write it fancy or draw some pictures to help you remember it even better.

_____

_____

_____

Keep Learning!

We have talked about some of the most important names of Jesus in this book, but you can always keep learning more about Jesus. He has many, many more names. In fact, the names of Jesus are found everywhere throughout the Bible!

There are so many names of Jesus that I had to pick only a few for us to learn about together! From start to finish in the Bible, everywhere you look, you can discover Jesus. *Everywhere!*

There's something awesome about the name of Jesus. So make sure you call Him by name and share His name with others as you tell them all about your amazing Savior!

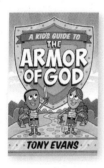

To learn more about Harvest House books and
to read sample chapters, visit our website:

www.harvesthousepublishers.com

HARVEST HOUSE PUBLISHERS
EUGENE, OREGON